Yet a Stranger

Yet a Stranger

Why Black Americans Still Don't Feel at Home

Deborah Mathis

WARNER BOOKS

An AOL Time Warner Company

Warner Books, Inc., 1271 Avenue of the Americas, New York, NY 10020

Visit our Web site at www.twbookmark.com.

For information on Time Warner Trade Publishing's online publishing program,
visit www.ipublish.com.

W An AOL Time Warner Company

Printed in the United States of America

First Printing: May 2002
10 9 8 7 6 5 4 3 2 1

Library of Congress Cataloging-in-Publication Data
Mathis, Deborah.
    Yet a stranger : why Black Americans still don't feel at home / Deborah Mathis.
        p. cm.
    ISBN 0-446-52636-3
    1. African Americans—Social conditions. 2. African Americans—Civil rights. 3. African
Americans—Psychology. 4. United States—Race relations. 5. Racism—United States. I.
Title.

    E185.86 .M3828 2002
    305.896'073—dc21   2001046641

Book design by Charles Sutherland

For my children,
Meredith, Allison, and Joseph,
whose love is my refuge and strength.

Acknowledgments

My late friend Willie Morris, that great writer and southern swain, once told me that writing a book is a misery. All the while, he urged me to get to it, aware that I had that fire that all would-be authors have and that if I didn't let the book—and the fire—out of me, the anguish of *not* writing would consume me. Either way, it seemed, I was doomed. But getting started seemed impossible. Willie assured me I would know when the time was right and that even then I might resist. "But do it," he said. "Do it till you get it done."

One day in 1999, a sweet-voiced woman named Caroline Carney, a Chicago-based literary agent, called me at work. She told me she had been reading my syndicated columns and wondered whether I had ever written a book, whether I was writing a book now, or whether I was interested in ever writing a book. Her call came out of the blue, which, to me, signaled divine dispatch. God had sent an angel to extinguish the fire.

In short order, the idea for this book was formalized. Its title, *Yet a Stranger*, is derived from the "stranger in two worlds" passage in W.E.B. DuBois's magnificent work *The Souls of Black Folk*. Having recently re-read DuBois's book, I was struck by how much had changed for black Americans since his assessment of Negro life at the opening of the twentieth century. And how much had not. I thought it was appropriate to take another look at black life in the world's richest, freest, and most powerful country at the dawn of the twenty-first century.

The research was long and complicated, but fun: I enjoyed digging into history, commentary, and analysis. I enjoyed recalling my own experiences. I really enjoyed talking about the book.

But writing it, as Willie had cautioned, was indeed a miserable, painstaking, mind-blowing enterprise. Transferring a series of ideas, recollections, and data from mind to paper in a way that makes sense, that flows, that delivers the goods is crushing work. Furthermore, even when I wasn't hunched over the computer keyboard, the fledgling book was dancing or stumbling or flailing in my head. Everything I saw or did, everyone I spoke with, everywhere I went seemed to be sending messages about something to add or change or delete. There were many a moment when I wondered why I hadn't just stuck to my day job.

Thankfully, there were other things in my head too—namely the voices of people who believed in me and in what I was doing: Willie, who left us before I finished the book. Caroline, who never seemed to have a whit of doubt that I could, and should, do it and who became a cherished friend. My editors at Warner: Anita Diggs, whose enthusiasm for the book was boundless. Betsy Mitchell, who showed me immediately that I didn't have to sell her on the merits of the book and whose steady eye and hand were invaluable. Jessica Papin, whose support buoyed me and affirmed my work. Warner publisher Jamie Raab, who treated me like a "natural" at writing from the start. And Bob Castillo, managing editor at Warner, who was so patient and helpful that, for a time, I thought I might be his only author.

Needless to say, I am forever grateful to my mother, sister, brothers and their spouses, nephews and nieces who fill my life with laughter and purge it of pretense. I am also indebted to my colleagues at Gannet News Service who put up with my endless chatter and preoccupations about the book; my bosom buddies David Judson and the remarkable Karyne Conley who did all the bragging for me and whisked me off for dinner and wine when they thought I got too uptight and wouldn't leave the house; the fabulous Dr. Ray Winbush, a brilliant scholar and author, who talked up my book even while it was in incubation and while he was on his own book tour.

No mother ever had finer children than mine, the helplessly devoted Meredith, Allison, and Joseph, who did not complain when their mother went into hiding for days at a time, only to emerge looking like human hazardous waste—hungry, disoriented, and worn. Their support, good humor, and faith never faltered. Their pride kept me going. Their love sustained me.

And I must give praise to my God, who has been ridiculously good to me all of my days. He has blessed me with the love of family and good health and has gifted me with a call to service, a love for humanity, and the inspiration and talent to write. Not for a moment have I deserved such bounty. I am living proof that He is almighty and all good.

I am, of course, happy to be writing this now, as the book is done. I pray that it makes a difference. A profit would be nice too, but a difference is more important.

I am proud of this accomplishment. Writing it was a misery, indeed. But such a splendid one.

Contents

Yet a Stranger

Chapter 1

Which Way to the Promised Land?

I love the old girl despite her nasty ways. I know she needs me. I think she knows it too. Still, she can be so difficult at times. So ornery and ungrateful. Cruel on occasion. Wicked. Inflicting pain and tribulation just for the heck of it, it seems. Yet every time, just as I am about to collapse under her tiresome demands or explode with rage from her abuse, she pulls me to her bosom and rocks me with promises. One moment I am her curse, the next her beloved.

I am determined to get her well even though she can be a most uncooperative patient, refusing to come clean about the seriousness of her ailments; refusing to settle down for the serious therapy she needs. Her mercurial nature repels me today, attracts me tomorrow, but always, always intrigues. Of course I realize her neurosis is dangerous and that I should probably run off. That would show her. But I am a sucker for the good in her, which is a good too good to leave. So here I stay, battered but bewitched. What can I say? She is my country, my home.

Four centuries have lapsed since the first twenty Africans were wrenched from their families, their land, their language, their customs, and altogether their freedom, then shipped across the treacherous Atlantic and delivered into the clutches of English settlers at Jamestown, Virginia. Four hundred years. Enough time, you would think, to have come to terms with such a patently grievous wrong—to have not only abolished the heinous institution of slavery, but to have eradicated every vile thought, every ignorant theory, every wicked impulse that gave rise to and nurtured the practice. Enough time to have taken every measure available and imaginable to repair the breach between black and white and to reconcile us, American to American.

Yet black Americans, descendants of the stolen Africans, still do not have equal footing with white Americans who share with us a nation. This is our home, but we do not enjoy its full range of comforts.

Like strangers, we are less at ease, transacting our daily lives with less true liberty, more trepidation, and in the face of more closed or stubborn doors than others who call America home. We are by no means newcomers, nor are our numbers so slight that the disparities can be excused as oversights. The original twenty have become thirty-five million souls. Most of us—91 percent—were born and have lived only here.

Still, from time to time and in sundry ways, come signs that our presence is not welcomed. The United States of America may be our home and, as such, it deserves our duty—our productivity, patriotism, and compliance. But it does not always *feel* like home.

Not if home is where you let your hair down and kick your shoes off and help yourself to the bounty. Not if home is where you don't have to tiptoe or look over your shoulder or wonder what they're saying about you or doing behind your back. Not if home is where there are no favorites, only equal kin. Not if home is where the others care about you and wouldn't think of letting you go hungry or homeless or ill-educated or without medical care, without nurturance of, or appreciation for, the gifts you bring and the talents with which you are endowed. Not if home is where it is one for all and all for one. Not if home is where you need not explain yourself as if you are some mystery created for intrigue or dissection—"a chronic patient for the sociological clinic, the sick man of American democracy," as black writer Alain Locke put it in 1925.

There is an absence of hospitality, a distance, a hesitation, a suspiciousness directed at black Americans that is unbecoming of a place called home. Instead there exists the sense of being on shaky ground, the awareness of hostility and confrontation bubbling just beneath the surface. A feeling that at any moment the little dance of tolerance may be abandoned and there you'd have it: a full frontal assault of prejudice, fear, anger, and deadly assumptions even though, these days, the attack may be so subtle and shifty that it is difficult for even the beholder to discern, let alone for its targets to indict. It is, in its modern form, what might be called "passive racism."

In his 1968 treatise, *The New Racialism,* Harvard professor Daniel Patrick Moynihan—later a U.S. senator from New York—adopted a new terminology for racial prejudice. While acknowledging "a streak of the racist virus in the American bloodstream," Moynihan chose to distinguish the more common strain as "racialism." It was a phenomenon, he said, "a profoundly different position from that of racism, with its logic of genocide and subordination. And it does no service whatever to this polity to identify as racist attitudes that which are merely racialist and which will, usually, on examination, be found to have essentially a social class basis." Moynihan may have been on to something. Not that the distinction dulls the pain.

Three decades later, the National Report Card on Discrimination made another effort at distinguishing between active and passive racism, naming the latter "Have-A-Nice-Day" discrimination. More critical and insightful than Moynihan regarding the perniciousness of this passive strain of race prejudice, the Report Card authors warned of its deceit in fostering "premature claims that we have achieved a color-blind society."

But worse than that, passive racism, racialism, Have-A-Nice-Day discrimination—call it what you will—denies its heritage. It overlooks the connection between itself, which tolerates disparity and injustice, and active racism, which often explodes into invective, intimidation, and violence. As it did on June 14, 1998, in the small town of Jasper, Texas.

That is where they found James Byrd's keys, his dentures, his head, and his torso, each in a separate spot along a three-mile stretch of Huff Creek Road. Byrd's killers, all young white men, had picked up the black man in town and driven him to the outskirts where they beat him, hitched him to the bumper of their pickup truck with a towing chain, and dragged him literally to pieces, apparently for the thrill of it.

Other racial atrocities marked America's approach to her fourth century of black and white cohabitation at the dawn of the third millennium. A Haitian immigrant was beaten and sodomized by a white New York City police officer. In the same city, a black man, standing in the doorway of his apartment building and holding only his wallet, was gunned down by four white cops who fired forty-one bullets, hitting flesh and bone nineteen times. Pipe bombs accompanied by racist threats shook up a historically black university in Florida. In suburban Chicago, a black basketball coach on an after-dinner stroll with two of his four young children was fatally shot by an avowed white separatist itching for a race war. A black teenager on his way home was killed for sport by two white boys in Indiana. In Los Angeles, three racist "skinheads" kicked and beat a homeless man to death because he was black. Black students and faculty at the University of Maryland were rattled for weeks by a rash of death threats. An African immigrant was gunned down at a bus stop in Denver, chosen randomly by young white men who claimed to be "race warriors." Three white American soldiers stationed at Fort Bragg, North Carolina, shot and killed a black couple walking down the street in order to earn the skinheads' medal for killing blacks—a spiderweb tattoo. The Los Angeles Police Department discovered a sinister hive in its Ramparts Division wherein officers had framed, beaten, threatened, and even kidnapped and shot scores of suspects, most of them black and brown men.

In every case, expressions of shock and condemnation poured from every corner, irrespective of race. But outside local protests, no real alarms were sounded. There was no sustained outrage, no urgent appeals to dig up the hows and whys of the many race-based tragedies that momentarily shook the New Age. It was generally accepted that the incidents were isolated and anomalous, far different from the epidemic of black lynchings, stake-burnings, and drownings that had bedeviled the early twentieth century. Since widespread racial terrorism no longer presented a constant danger, the nation, though horrified and aggrieved by each awful modern instance, was able to dismiss the tragedies and the perpetrators as aberrations—a nasty but temporary rash on the body politic rather than a serious and festering disease. The more extreme the racist violence, the easier it was for earnestly appalled whites to denounce it without having to acknowledge, or even examine, its relationship to common prejudices ingrained in daily life.

Instead, they drew satisfaction from outward signs and their own good behavior. They did not use the "n" word; they lived near, worked and socialized with black people; they contributed cheerfully to the Black College Fund or the Sickle Cell Anemia Foundation; they were counted among the fans of black entertainers, writers, and athletes; they allowed their children to sleep over at black friends' houses. But these snapshots of interracial harmony are an illusion. Americans' shrugging indifference to continuing, long-lived social disparities tells the real story.

After all, racism has always been about substance, not style. In the 1950s, much of my native Arkansas was charmed by such a man. His name was Jim Johnson. In 1956 he sought the Democratic nomination for governor. Johnson was a man with an engaging smile. Well-read, handy with a pen, and pedantic about history and literature, Johnson fancied himself something of an intellectual and the beau ideal of southern gentlemanliness. But his love of the classics and his social graces could not mask his writhing racism. One of the reasons he wanted to be governor was that he found Orval Faubus too Negro-friendly—the same Orval Faubus who would later defy the U.S. Supreme Court and the president of the United States on school desegregation. During the 1956 campaign, Johnson appealed to fellow bigots by refusing to shake a black person's hand along the campaign trail. He lost the nomination that year, but two years later Johnson wormed his way into the voters' good graces and took a seat on the Arkansas Supreme Court, his racism intact and in tow.

These days, few supremacists can afford to be as direct as Johnson or his midcentury peers. The contemporary crowd is more artful in speech and tactics. Take Charlton Heston, an actor who portrayed some of the greats of history, from Moses to Michelangelo. But in the 1990s, Heston fell in with the National Rifle Association and, in short order, became the gun lobby's president and its most celebrated spokesman.

Speaking to the archconservative Free Congress Foundation in 1997, Heston presented a message distinguishable from what any snaggle-toothed white supremacist might say only because it was delivered with Heston's inimitable dramatic flair.

"The Constitution was handed down to guide us by a bunch of those wise old dead white guys who invented this country," Heston told his audience.

Now, some flinch when I say that. Why? It's true . . . they were white guys. So were most of the guys who died in Lincoln's name opposing slavery in the 1860s. So why should I be ashamed of white guys? Why is "Hispanic pride" or "black pride" a good thing while "white pride" conjures up shaved heads and white hoods? Why was the Million Man March on Washington celebrated in the media as progress while the Promise Keepers March on Washington was greeted with suspicion and ridicule? I'll tell you why—cultural warfare.

Then, in a nostalgic vein, Heston said good citizens "prefer the America they built, where you could pray without feeling naïve, love without being kinky, sing without profanity, be white without feeling guilty, own a gun without shame and raise your hand without apology." And "Heaven help the God-fearing, law-abiding, Caucasian, middle class Protestant." At that point, Heston called up his civil rights bona fides—a sophisticated version of the "some-of-my-best-friends" tack.

"In 1963, I marched on Washington with Dr. Martin Luther King to uphold the Bill of Rights," Heston thundered. Then he denounced "blacks who raise a militant fist with one hand while they seek preference with the other." But Heston apparently had no problem with white actors who extol racial harmony one moment and stick a knife in it the next.

Whether Heston always had a split personality on race or was converted to bigotry late in life will be his secret. But, had he been an apprentice of modern racism in need of propaganda, he would not have had to rummage through dusty annals to find it. New material is plentiful, filling bookshelves, newsstands, and, most especially, the Internet with its explosion of supremacist web sites. By 2001, the Southern Poverty Law Center in Montgomery, Alabama, was tracking more than six hundred such sites. Many were organs of real life, flesh-and-blood hate groups, some with chapters in several states.

For inspiration, they may turn to Glayde Whitney, a psychology professor at Florida State University. In an interview with the

Associated Press, Whitney bewailed the country's attempts to install and uphold equality because, he said, biology defies it. Black people, he said, are "mentally not very smart" and should just give up on the quest for parity.

Within mainstream society, there has been an astonishing lack of resistance to proclamations like Whitney's or those of another academic, Charles Murray, coauthor of *The Bell Curve: Intelligence and Class Structure in American Life.* Far from being spurned, Murray's book floated on the *New York Times* best-seller list for weeks, with the author lapping up acclaim and fat fees on the lecture and talk show circuits. (Murray's coauthor, Richard J. Hernstein, died before the book was published in 1994.)

The popularity of literature and so-called science that are degrading to people of color keeps faith with a timeless American tradition. In his *Notes on the State of Virginia*, written in 1781–82, Thomas Jefferson attached a litany of stereotypes, myths, and lies to black people, providing an ideological boilerplate for modern prejudices:

> *The first difference which strikes us is that of colour. Whether the black of the negro resides in the reticular membrane between the skin and scarf-skin, or in the scarf-skin itself; whether it proceeds from the colour of the blood, the colour of the bile, or from that of some other secretion, the difference is fixed in nature, and is as real as if its seat and cause were better known to us. And is this difference of no importance? Is it not the foundation of a greater or less share of beauty in the two races? Are not the fine mixtures of red and white, the expressions of every passion by greater or less suffusions of colour in the one, preferable to that external monotony,*

which reigns in the countenances, that immovable veil of black which covers all the emotions of the other race?

"Confounding father" that he was, Jefferson concluded that "the blacks, whether originally a distinct race, or made distinct by time and circumstances, are inferior to the whites in the endowments both of body and mind." He attributed an array of behaviors and proclivities to blackness, including inordinate perspiration, little need for sleep, bravery and adventuresomeness, an ability to quickly get over affliction and grief, an intolerance for cold temperatures, and sexual intensity—though "love seems with them to be more an eager desire than a tender delicate mixture of sentiment and sensation." Perhaps that is why Jefferson repeatedly had sex with his slave, the lovely Sally Hemmings, but failed to behave lovingly toward her or the children they allegedly produced together, not even enough to set them free.

Most white Americans today might reject Jefferson's assertions, but in some cases, it would be for their particulars, not the overarching point of Jefferson's dissertation on race. The sense of white superiority, if not supremacy—of entitlement, of preference, of ownership, of priority—remains whole and prosperous. It is deeply occulted in the American mind, a mind that, according to Alain Locke, regards the black American as "more of a formula than a human being—a 'something' to be argued about, condemned or defended, to be 'kept down' or 'in his place' or 'helped up,' to be worried with or worried over, harassed or patronized, a social bogey or a social burden." Often, even the most conscientious whites think of themselves as reaching down rather than reaching out when they come to the aid of their black countrymen.

Verily, the nation is well along in mastering the rituals and trappings of equality. But it has yet to embrace its genuine, or spiritual, objective, which is the equalization of opportunity and stature, regardless of color. Despite measurable, even monumental, gains in categories like income, education, and the enlargement of the black middle class, life for the multitude of black Americans is not much different from the way it was in 1944 when Swedish economist Gunnar Myrdal wrote his groundbreaking book, *An American Dilemma.* "The Negroes do not by far have anything approaching a tenth of the things worth having in America," wrote Myrdal. Today millions of black Americans can see no way out of the destitution described by Myrdal six decades ago.

In fact, most black American children remain confined to resegregated, poorly equipped schools that have been drained of financial and moral support. Millions of black Americans are quarantined in decrepit public housing projects, consigned to minimum wage jobs at the end of a broom or a drive-through window. One of every three young black males is, or has been, in prison. The New Age, the Communications Age, the Information Age are not accessible to many black Americans. Overall, the ranks of black Americans who are cut off from the mainstream are, as ever, legion. They are all but doomed to languish and waste away in a world where only producers and "haves" count. Escape is possible, but it usually requires exceptional fortitude, a stroke of good luck, uncommon patience, and soul-sapping perseverance—all admirable and good but such exceptional and inordinate requirements, compared to what other Americans expend for the same prize, the same destination.

Americans may be accustomed to the disparities and double

standards that color American life, but they are detestable and, truth be told, inexcusable. Good intentions do not suffice, nor does moralizing. The popular refrain that "personal responsibility" alone can undo the damage or level the playing field is born of high arrogance and ignorance. So is the "Super Negro" factor, which offers a shot at the American Dream after a black man, woman, or child has invested more talent, wit, and will than is ordinarily or rightly required. Furthermore, we are offended by suggestions that we should be meek and grateful that things are not as bad as they once were. Given the gaping differences between the prospects for a white American child and a black American child, we take no comfort in comparisons to how it used to be or how it might be still. Our sights are set on how it should be and how it should have been all along.

Chapter 2

What More Do You People Want?

The flagrantly racist acts and policies that stain much of American history provide a certain service in that they are unambiguous. "Whites only" signs require no interpretation or discernment. However ridiculous and offensive the old-fashioned tactics and systems of racism were, they were at least straightforward. They were at least—and it pains me to apply this term to such evil, but—*honest.* It was not difficult to size up the enemy in those days.

Rather than physical danger and harsh confrontation, the new common threat to the peace and prosperity of black Americans is a steady diet of indignities, disillusions, rejections, and suspicions that poison our hope, our patriotism, and our ambition. However, much of white America does not want to hear this complaint. Things are better, they declare—by every account, by any book, they have improved. They believe the 1964 Civil Rights Act, the

1965 Voting Rights Act, the proliferation of affirmative action policies, and expansive desegregation neutralized any grievances black America has about access and opportunity. Therefore, disparities that exist in income, educational attainment, and life expectancy are imaginary, greatly exaggerated, or our fault, so goes the standard spin. Believing they have ceded plenty for our sakes and in the name of equalization, doubters harbor a roiling resentment and fatigue, often encased in one famous question: What more do you people want?

The question is, of course, ludicrous and rhetorical, designed to make a statement and not solicit an answer. Those who ask it are stating, in effect, that we have overstepped our bounds, outstayed our welcome, exhausted geniality and accommodation, been overindulged and, in the process, proven ourselves to be an insatiable, greedy lot, expecting more than we have any right to ask. *What more do you people want?*

The virus of resentment and fatigue may be at large in the white community. Some of the people afflicted with it are troubled by how they've started thinking about black people and the entire equality question. Several have called me in my capacity as a newspaper columnist, seeking relief from the awful ideas that are beginning to swell in their heads. Invariably, these callers tell me that they are well educated, have enjoyed interracial friendships, have never considered themselves to be a bigot or a racist but fret that "I'm becoming one." Their reasons are usually presented with more civility and forethought than those of the occasional raging racist who writes or calls. But there is little difference in the essence of what they have to say. In either case, the argument comes down to this: Black people have as many opportunities as any other American to be healthy, safe, educated, employed, and prosperous. So, if we have babies out of wedlock, do poorly in school, end up in prison or too early in the grave, sell drugs, use crack, have dead-end jobs, and otherwise exist on life's dingy, risky, outer rim, why should white Americans have to be accountable for it, subsidize it, defer to it, apologize for it, or even worry about it? And what in the world does the long-gone institution of slavery have to do with present conditions and circumstances? After all of the loftily worded laws, the constitutional tinkering, the shared facilities, the ceded ground, the proliferation of interracial friendships and love affairs, an "Administration that looks like America"—after all this, they ask WHAT MORE DO YOU PEOPLE WANT?

More than their own exhaustion and frustration, the protestors betray a deep misunderstanding of black America and an underestimation of history's long-term effects. Except during outbreaks of vicious bigotry, it is difficult to persuade white America that the alienation of black America is actual and ongoing, afflicting each generation through policy, custom, quack science, and, if nothing else, the Look.

We learn to recognize the Look very early in life. It radiates from white strangers' faces. It's not the same look of benign curiosity that is cast upon the typical newcomer, but a distinct look of unease, confusion, dislike, disapproval, alarm, dread, even hatred. And it conveys myriad questions—What are you doing here? What do you want? What are you up to?—while making one unmistakable appeal: go away.

It is impossible to describe the Look to those outside its range. Sometimes, I'm sure, the transmitter is hardly aware he or she has dispatched it. But black people can feel it as sharply as the cutting wind and have learned to anticipate it, though the Look occasionally catches us off guard. If you are hit by it early in life or often enough, the Look can kill. Not your body, but your spirit. Kill your faith that you will ever belong. Kill your hopes that what you have to offer the world will ever be noticed, appreciated, nurtured, or rewarded. Kill your desire to participate, to go along, to get along. Snuff out your will to even try.

How frequently we encounter the Look depends, in part, on where we live and do business, the cast of our skin and how much or little we reflect white norms and customs in the way we walk, talk, and dress. Blacks in the upper economic strata, especially those who dress conservatively and are well established in the American mainstream, will get the Look less often than those who are poor and less well versed in Anglo-American standards. Males who are poor and black are likely to be snared by the Look so often and harshly that the Look leaves a stab wound.

Every self-aware black American knows the Look and its cruel implications. Even those who have attempted to shed all vestiges of their blackness experience it from time to time when they arrive on unfamiliar turf before their résumés or portfolios have been introduced and they are just another black stranger to be warily surveyed.

For the most part, we are spared this offense in our earliest years. As infants and toddlers, we either pass unnoticed by strangers or are treated benignly, being too young to rouse suspicion or fear. But by the time the natural rambunctiousness of youth takes hold and we begin to act and think independently, the Look begins to land on us, raising that sense of "otherness" that black people have been writing and talking about ever since Africa lost its treasure to these shores. Black educators and social workers have traced the onset of this phenomenon to about age nine. They call it "the fourth-grade hook" to mark the turning point from assumed innocent sprite to presumed developing menace. After that, the Look gradually becomes more frequent, harder and more corrosive, supplanting the presumption of innocence with the anticipation of criminality, depravity, and incompetence. It yokes the child with self-doubt, intimidation, and a definite sense of unwelcomeness, a sense of strangeness, even in his own home country. In response, the black child may become more careful and self-conscious, more cunning, or more reckless and rebellious. Whatever the response, it is a strain against the psychic chains that would bind his sense of self-worth, liberty, belonging, and happiness.

The Look is a draining thing, but there are countermeasures. One is to ignore it, to starve it of feedback. Another is to meet it with a defiant stare and rigid stance, daring the Look to turn into words or action. A third approach is to defuse the Look with broad smiles, humor, an ostentatious display of etiquette and articulation, an overdone geniality, even self-effacement—the Anti-Menace routine. We learn to command these strategies early and can conjure them reflexively. What a pitiful state of affairs it is that any American should need such a repertoire. Consider this example:

Three black teenage boys stand at a convenience store checkout counter. They are wearing the uniform of their generation: baggy pants, long T-shirts, sloppy unlaced sneakers, and, on one, a baseball cap turned backward. The clerk, a middle-aged white woman, is scowling, cutting her eyes at the teens as she serves an elderly man at the counter. When the man leaves, the first teen steps up, places a bag of chips, a soft drink, and two candy bars on the counter. He digs into his pockets for cash. The clerk snarls, "Would you wait a minute?" then mumbles something laced with disdain.

Immediately, the play unfolds. The boy widens his eyes, relaxes his jaw, and says nervously, "Oh, sorry." He scoops his goods from the counter. Behind him, his friend drops his head and gazes at the floor. The last one stares into the distance, his mouth taut, his gleamless eyes fixed and unblinking. He seems tired—sick and tired, no doubt—of a look he has seen too many times. He can't be more than sixteen years old.

Imagine that kind of reception day in, day out. In school. On the streets. At the mall. *What are you doing here? What are you up to?* Imagine being sized up and discarded on the basis of the way you walk or talk or dress or joke around. Imagine how it eats away at your joy and may eventually chew on your own goodness. Stab wounds.

At its worst, the Look threatens greater offenses—oppressive, discriminatory, and presumptuous acts, policies, practices, and laws based on assumptions. It assumes black Americans have not only a unique American experience and perspective but a distinct essence. A lesser essence. Those who don't know us believe we possess a different temperament and different natural urges, and that we lack intellectual or moral altitude, that we are by nature needy and dependent. Hence, our successes are often measured in dollars and degrees and are met with celebration and wonder as to what miracle—or what savior—intervened to lift us from our sorry original state. For many, we are still a curiosity. Even in our own country. Even at home.

White confusion over the constancy of black agitation and protest is understandable when one recognizes their unfamiliarity with the day-to-day dynamics of black life. What they see is that the first and most brazen constructs of institutional racism—slavery and segregation—have been dismantled. What even the most sensitive and sympathetic whites cannot see or know is the extent and depth of our exposure to attitudinal racism or the stubbornness of its grip or the profundity of its effects on us. The racial divide is real. It is measurable by statistical disparities in poverty, crime, scholastic achievement, health, and longevity. But it is there in the abstract too—in the lost faith and security of those who have been repeatedly scalded by the Look.

Chapter 3

Fire, What Fire?

Amerita has staked her claim to racial harmony on the muddy ground of relativity. What *used to be,* compared to what *is.* How bad it *could be* rather than how bad it *is.* On this basis, the country has declared itself healed. It has proclaimed color blindness. It has set the past aside and forgiven itself. It is better than it used to be, not as bad as it could be, goes the rationale.

But it is self-deception to believe that the comparisons are satisfying. It's also risky, leaving the nation unprepared and shocked when the deception collapses. That happens every now and then. It happened one afternoon in Los Angeles, the City of Angels. All hell broke loose. On that day in the spring of 1992, the anger, fears and frustrations of the ages bore down on a single event and black Americans spilled into the streets in a fit of ENOUGH!

Outside Los Angeles, far from the South Central pocket where the city's poorest lived, a white jury had acquitted four white police officers of beating a black motorist named Rodney King. The entire country, indeed the world, had seen replay after replay of an amateur videotape of the beating in which more than a dozen officers set upon King with their nightsticks as he lay curled on the ground. For black Americans, particularly black men, the existence of a videotape had been something to celebrate, its disturbing content notwithstanding. For generations, black people had complained, marched, sued, and screamed about police brutality, only to encounter denial, disbelief, and the proverbial "blue wall of silence"—the unwritten pact among law enforcement officials to say and do nothing that incriminates a fellow officer. Here for once was undeniable proof caught by the unblinking eye of a camera.

Certainly the police officers, reminiscent of the plantation bosses of yore, had shown no hesitation in their attack on King. As Sgt. Stacey Koon would testify in a federal civil rights trial in the case: "The intent was to cripple, to disable Rodney King, to break his bones." The officers involved said they had to resort to violence because King was out of control, possibly under the influence of hallucinogenic drugs and difficult to subdue. But to the average person watching the videotape that was played incessantly on every newscast in the country, King seemed only to be trying to get to his feet.

When Koon, Officer Laurence Powell and two other policemen were tried on assault charges in Simi Valley—a conservative, predominantly white enclave thirty-five miles away—the city of Los Angeles crackled with tension and speculation over the verdict and its implications. Conviction seemed foregone, and every black man who had ever been accosted by the police got a whiff of justice in the air. "When Rodney King was on the ground getting beat, we were all on the ground getting beat," said the Reverend Floyd Flake, then a Democratic congressman from New York.

On April 29, 1992, a jury of ten whites, one Asian, and one Latino issued a verdict that split what tender seams had held the city's peace: All of the officers were acquitted. As dusk fell on Los Angeles and word of the verdict spread, predominantly black and Latino South Central L.A. exploded in violence. The area became a movie set of mayhem, with fires, looting, beatings, and gunfire. To the rioters, justice, so often slapped around, had this time been smashed to smithereens. If King, backed by the graphic videotape, could not expect justice then what black man could?

Hundreds of miles away in Jackson, Mississippi, I too was on fire with shock and rage the morning after the jury's decision. That day, I was scheduled to participate in a panel discussion about management and public relations for a group of state employees. The audience of forty or so black and white workers was not prepared for what I had to say.

"Last night, a jury in southern California found four white police officers not guilty of assaulting Rodney King," I began. "This morning, South Central L.A. is burning." The audience nodded knowingly, then waited for what I am sure they thought would be my reproof. I steadied my eye. "As I told my husband this morning," I continued, "I'm afraid that if I were in L.A. last night or this morning, I'd be right out there with them, burning that sucker down."

It was as if the nerves in the room had been abruptly exposed. You could feel them writhing, raw and irritated, aggravated by this unexpected invasion.

I do not condone violence but, Lord knows, I often understand its impulses. That is what I wanted to convey that April morning, despite my digression from the day's agenda. The fury and passion simply overwhelmed me so that I wanted somehow to strike out too, to be in on the eruption, to put white America on notice that the security, calmness, and control they crave were neither solid nor guaranteed. I wanted them to know that the city of Los Angeles, the state of California, the United States itself is built upon a racial fault line that may hold together for long spells but which is bound to crack open. On that day, I did not mind being impertinent, shocking, infuriating, and radical, which is precisely how some of the meeting's attendants found me, according to their subsequent letters of protest and outrage. All one angry writer could muster was that I had been "unprofessional."

Perhaps my critics shared the sentiments of one King juror, as reported by *USA Today* shortly after the riots began. The rioters were not upset by the verdict, she surmised. "They were just waiting for something to happen so they could go out."

Here, once more, was the notion that black people have no justifiable grievances, no long-lasting, unresolved, and serious plaints. That sentiment ignores our long-suffering history and our habitual patience. It belittles our credibility. It challenges our right to complain. It concludes that our rebellion can only be a function of an innate savagery, a predisposition to upset and destroy, an inability to control ourselves, a refusal to conform. Much of this comes from people who celebrate the Whiskey Rebellion, the Haymarket Square Riot, Lexington and Concord, and the Civil War as righteous acts of the utmost patriotic urgency—examples of American-style grit and courage in the face of untenable conditions. But when black Americans push against unfairness, we are thought to be simply craven—spoiling for a fight, waiting for something to happen.

I will concede that my angry exposition may have been out of place on that morning. But, like the rioters, I needed so badly to release some of the pent-up frustration that the appropriateness of time, place, and method, or lack thereof, did not faze me. Like the South Central actors, I wanted to upset the white folks, to get their attention, and to make them uncomfortable on their perches of privilege. From my safe distance, I found the chaos intoxicating and, in a way, rejuvenating. Insurrection, even when failed and futile, is a sign that the oppressed have not given up, that they have not accepted a place on life's low rungs, that they see themselves as sovereign, consecrated, God-made individuals with all the inalienable rights thereto entitled, and that they recognize the injustice and fallacy of the system that oppresses them and that, yes, they will be heard.

Notwithstanding my rantings, I tried to tie together the verdict aftermath and the topic the workshop organizers had asked me to address: how government offices might improve communications with the public in general and the news media specifically. I had a difficult time staying focused and I feel quite sure the workshop participants felt I had cheated them out of the career advice they had come for. Normally, it would have bothered me to think I had disappointed an audience. But what mattered to me most that day, rightly or wrongly, was letting white Americans know that, as a power class, they should not feel so snug in their nests today.

Four years later, on a business trip to Los Angeles, I got into a conversation with an airport shuttle driver. How is the rebuilding effort going, I wanted to know. Not well, the driver said. Seems the sense of urgency that once gripped the city and set a lot of balls in motion had relaxed considerably. It was back to business as usual, he said.

"But, for about three or four months after the riots," he added, "man, we were in charge. White folks were so nice and friendly and respectful. Of course we knew that meant they were scared, but it didn't matter. It was just good to have that power for a change."

I knew what he meant. But when people are so deprived of common kindnesses and so accustomed to being hassled and harassed or ignored and rejected, when they have such hunger for recognition that their egos are satisfied by gratuitous, self-serving, and insincere shows of respect, no wonder they are not picky about the reason behind the attention. What a sad way for home to be.

Chapter 4

Say It Ain't So

The South Central Los Angeles riots of 1992 were no minor event. There were fifty-three deaths. More than two thousand injuries were reported. Property damage was assessed at one billion dollars. Commissions were established to decide how to put the city back together. A slew of social architects got to work and a few of the rioters were put on trial. Ultimately, however, the country dismissed the riots as spontaneous, meaningless violence, undirected and unspecified anger for which the King verdict had been only an excuse.

Certainly it is commendable that the country always gets over its troubles and moves on with life. But when the trouble is recurring, you have to wonder when the country is going to rip the scab off its wounds and carve out the infection. How many times must racial conflict turn swollen and feverish before America admits it has a serious malady?

Moving on beyond the L.A. riots was precisely what America intended to do—what it thought it had done—when the disease once more rose out of remission. It started, once again, in a California courtroom. This time, a predominantly black jury in Los Angeles acquitted a black football hero on charges of murdering his ex-wife and her friend, both white.

For its legal significance, the O.J. Simpson murder trial may not have been "the trial of the century," as it was billed almost from the start. But culturally, there was hardly a more momentous case than that of the handsome, hulking former football star and media gadabout. A nation seemingly bored with common violence was at once repulsed and attracted in the summer of 1994, when Simpson was charged with fatally slashing and stabbing the mother of his young children with such brutality that, in crime scene photos, Nicole Brown Simpson's head looked—as one juror put it—like a Pez dispenser. The other victim's youth, good looks, and bad timing—apparently Ronald Goldman came upon the scene during the attack on Nicole—only made the case more titillating. Black and white alike were mesmerized.

The case tapped a vein of public lust for thrills, suspense, and celebrity that burst open the night Simpson's white sports utility vehicle was spotted sailing down the Los Angeles freeways with a convoy of police cars in tow. The nation watched, via live television, to see what Simpson might do on the run. The man behind the wheel, Simpson's lifelong friend Al Cowling, told police that O.J. was distraught, armed and contemplating suicide. As word spread by TV and radio, motorists parked their cars on highway shoulders, overpasses, and exit ramps to watch the spectacle, cheering the Simpson vehicle as if it were the Super Bowl and the record-breaking running back, the one-time Heisman trophy winner, had the ball and was barreling toward the posts. Some had even taken the time to fashion signs that read, GO, O.J., GO.

It was not the first time the country had been captivated by a high-profile criminal case. It wasn't the only time folks had taken sides. Still, there was something unique about the Simpson case. Something that exposed a fascination with violence, an itch for sensationalism, a cynicism about the judicial process, a shamelessness about prying into the intimacies of strangers' private lives.

But in the final analysis, the resounding lesson from the case was what was *not* new, what had *not* changed in America—namely the gulf between whites and blacks. It was this unaltered state of interracial politics that left the most lasting impression.

By coincidence, a national conference on domestic violence was underway at a Washington, D.C., hotel on the day in October 1995 when the Simpson verdict was to be announced. The conference had been animated by testimony in the case related to Simpson's physical abuse of Nicole during their marriage. To follow up on the connection, I was assigned to cover the midday conference and gather reaction to the jury's decision. After a few skits, songs, and speeches decrying domestic violence and promoting prevention and prosecution of abusers, the conference was recessed minutes before the verdict reading. Women spilled into the hotel atrium where several large television sets had been stationed solely for the purpose of hearing the jury's call. Quickly, the lobbies filled with spectators—conference participants, hotel employees and guests, business types who were in the area for lunch or meetings, and passersby off the street. At that moment in America, everyone tuned in to O.J.

The way my heart pounded, head throbbed, and palms sweated, you'd have thought I cared something about the man. Not really. Oh, many years before I had been something of a fan, proud as all get-out of the California boy who made his name at the University of Southern California. I remember flushing with pride when that strong black form raced over the field, commanding yet another proving ground, scoring yet another victory for black achievement. I was happy for him when he landed in the pros. I watched him running through airports as a pitchman for Hertz, the rental car giant. I caught him a few times as an announcer of National Football League games and was happy to see that he was still moving forward. I had even felt good for him when he landed minor roles in minor movies, although his acting talents were modest, to say the least. He was part of the background of my life, someone who helped flesh out the good times.

But until they found Nicole Brown and Ronald Goldman lying in a lake of their own blood with wounds of immeasurable viciousness, and until they took the suspect down, I hadn't really thought of O.J. Simpson in years. My palpitations during the verdict watch would seem odd, then. Except everyone in the whole country had them and they didn't know him either. I was not sweating for O.J. per se, but for what he symbolized.

Over the course of the long trial, Simpson had come to represent something that mattered deeply and urgently to me: the unusual occasion of a criminally accused black man who was manipulating the system that so often manipulated black men. Of course, most black men did not have Simpson's means. Most could not call on some of the country's best and shrewdest lawyers and get them to drop everything and focus exclusively on a singular defense. Nor did they have the money to hire top-notch investigators, scientists, and other experts who knew the name of the game was Reasonable Doubt. Simpson's team specialized in creating it.

No ordinary black man accused of a crime, especially a violent one, had the resources to pursue a rumor that one of the lead detectives in the case was on record as loathing black people and therefore might have no reservations about setting up an innocent man. No typical black defendant could afford the time and money to track down an obscure writer who had the detective on audiotape, bragging about his malevolence toward people of color. No ordinary black man could have persuaded Henry Lee, a world-famous forensic scientist, to examine the evidence and then take the witness stand and hauntingly aver: "Something wrong."

That O.J. Simpson could muster all these advantages was testament, in part, to his seat at the table of uncommon privilege. There was a nagging sense that, to win that place, he had compromised some of himself, some of his blackness, maybe even forsaken some of it in order to appease the white world and gain passport to the good life. Simpson had no reputation for activism or philanthropy. Indeed, he seemed to have lived a life that most black people could only dream of. The consensus among black Americans was that O.J. was a brother by birth but no longer a brother in essence. So many people hoping for acquittal were not pulling for Simpson the black man as much as for the black man who happened to be Simpson.

On the other hand, many people earnestly believed in Simpson's innocence. They could not fathom that Simpson might have murdered someone, let alone his children's mother on the stoop of her home as the little ones slept upstairs. Some had problems with logistics. How could one person have unleashed such powerful rage? How could Simpson have done the deed, driven home, cleaned up, and caught a flight in what all parties agreed would have been a remarkably short amount of time? Others argued that the prosecution never established a motive.

Black observers, particularly, were skeptical of the charges because of the "dirty cop" scenario. Mark Fuhrman had a documented history of racist attitudes. He had already been caught in one big lie before the court, denying that he referred to black people as "niggers," when it was later proven Fuhrman had no qualms about using the word. For black people who were familiar with crooked cops and legal shenanigans, there was nothing far-fetched about the theory that Fuhrman had planted or tampered with evidence in order to incriminate Simpson. Fuhrman was all the reasonable doubt they needed. Something wrong, indeed.

As the trial wore on, much of white America became convinced of Simpson's guilt, particularly after hearing the powerful DNA evidence implicating him. As one lawyer put it in a post-trial analysis, one would have had to go to another planet to find a second match. Thus, in the face of the prosecution's "mountain of evidence," whites fully expected conviction, just as blacks had in the trial of Rodney King's tormentors. Whatever misgivings they had about some of the evidence and testimony, they were confident that a guilty verdict was the only sensible alternative. Mark Fuhrman's deviousness may have troubled whites, but the suggestion that he set Simpson up sounded more like a movie script than real life. They understood how people who believed it would favor acquittal. They just couldn't understand how anyone could believe it.

Meanwhile, many black Americans saw O.J.'s fate as being secondary to what the verdict would say about black America's claim on the benefit of doubt. To that group, the prospect of a black man's triumph over the same system that had shortchanged or shredded the rights of countless black men over generations was sweet comeuppance, long in coming, rare and precious. The prospect of acquittal was such a consolation to legions that it simply eclipsed the facts of whatever happened that awful night in Brentwood. White folks could not deal with that, which is why there was such an uneasy feeling in the hotel atrium with its smattering of black faces.

As we pressed toward the television sets, silence fell. Some people had their eyes closed and their fingers crossed. Others covered their mouths in nervous anticipation. A few clasped their hands as if in prayer. I swallowed hard as the clerk began reading the verdict. The cameras held tight on Simpson and his phalanx of powerful lawyers.

"We the jury in the above and titled action," began the clerk off-camera, "find the defendant, Oren . . ." She stumbled over his name, delaying the news by only seconds, but the crowd was pained by the pause. A fit of sighs and curses wafted through the atrium.

"Orenthal James Simpson," she continued, "not guilty—"

Instantly, my fist punched the air and a hissing "yes" escaped my mouth. I had not known what my reaction would be. I hadn't even been sure what I wanted to happen. But at that moment, relief and satisfaction swept over me like a cool tide and I was unable to contain my emotion despite my company, which, with little exception, was stricken. One young white woman standing next to

33

me was clearly perplexed by my reaction. She stared for a few seconds, seemingly horrified, and backed away. I scanned the area for similarly relieved faces and found two—one black, one Latino.

I quickly collected myself, pulled out my notepad and went to work, gathering reaction from the conferees. Though stunned, they gave cogent statements about the escalation of domestic violence, about misogyny, about the failure of the justice system to stop or punish abusers, about how men like O.J. are able to get away with abuse every day.

Finally, one of my subjects turned the tables on me. "I'm curious," she said. "What did *you* think?"

I hesitated. How could I explain it? How could I help her understand that, despite my misgivings about Simpson, I had known one too many black men who had been set up when no one believed it or no one had been able to prove it or no one had bothered to try. Was there time to tell her all the stories I'd heard, all the times I knew about a black man or boy being chased and frisked and made to lie with his face in the dirt? Should I tell her what I knew about false accusations and being trailed by store lookouts for absolutely no apparent reason other than blackness? Might she get it if I told her about the different worlds in which we live? Hers, with its entitlement and power, where white boys are groomed for executive suites, yachting, and managing their stock portfolios and where folks wonder what in the world went wrong when they miss the mark? Mine, with its constant demands to prove oneself worthy or competent or decent or innocent, where black boys feel they've accomplished something if they make it to twenty-five without having been jailed or killed? Where folks hold them up as some kind of freak when they do well? Could she possibly understand that I grieved for Nicole and Ronald, that I deplored what happened to them, that I am a law-and-order type, that I cannot dismiss the possibility of O.J.'s involvement and still, still, still, I am grateful that, this once, a reasonable doubt was not only raised but prevailed? Would she ever understand that it was not about O.J., that he was merely a stand-in, the Black Everyman, the Black Anyman?

There was no time for such deep diving.

"I'm just glad it's over," I said.

Speechless, the woman walked away.

Over the next several days, the fallout from the verdict began to settle in, to the shock and consternation of most whites. Across the country, television camera crews captured groups of blacks in celebration of the verdict. In college dorm rooms, in office buildings, at factories, on the street, throngs of blacks could be seen motionless except for heaving chests in anticipation of the verdict. Then, as Simpson's acquittal was announced, the bubble of silence exploded into cheers, applause, and shouts of joy. The woman who had asked me "What did you think?" got her answer.

It should be noted that not all black Americans favored the verdict. Nonetheless, political and social commentators took to their microphones and word processors to hammer both the jury's decision and those blacks who cheered Simpson's acquittal. Several accused Simpson's attorneys of "playing the race card." They accused the jury of using an individual criminal case to make a larger social statement about racial affairs. They called the jury ignorant and uncouth, challenging their fitness with the same sanctimony applied in defense of the white jurors in Simi Valley who had disregarded the videotaped beating of Rodney King and acquitted his attackers. They blasted the celebrants as irresponsible, nihilistic, and bearers of the double standard.

Overall, they missed the point. Not only did the analysts fail to grasp what Simpson represented to many black Americans—a black man who triumphed over the same system that had abused so many others—but it had not occurred to them that so many black Americans felt themselves abused. They did not understand that some of the cheering was honest relief for those who believed Simpson was both legally and literally not guilty. Nor did they pick up on people's pride in Johnnie Cochran's defense, pride in the black lawyer's triumph on an intellectual field of play. Talk of color blindness, diversity, and multiculturalism, buttressed by years of interracial mingling, had blurred their vision. They did not see that black anger was beginning to boil in the melting pot. They did not see the steam rising. Perhaps because they didn't know how to look at it. Perhaps because they didn't want to.

Justice is an integral ingredient to comfort at home. Without its warranty, no American can relax and go on about his or her way. None can feel at home.

Chapter 5

A Will and a Way

Persistent alienation and a sense of "otherness" do worse work than merely make black America feel lonely and dejected. They destroy spirit, kinship, and faith. The need for belonging and community is as fundamental to the human animal as the need to love and the need to believe in something greater than oneself. Deprived of them, a person's energies and talents can lose their sweetness and putrify. Take away my belonging and connectedness and you rob me of the sublime satisfaction of proving myself, the gratification of striving, the basic joy of dreaming. Without a community in which to display my goodness, I am exiled to the outskirts of society, untended and uncounted; the unheard tree, felled in the forest. Rather than being invited to bring whatever little I may have to put on the table, I am shoved aside, barred from partaking of more than what crumbs may fall to the floor. It is expected that, in return for these scraps, I will not make a fuss. Likewise, I must never complain about those who are seated for the feast. If, by chance, I should revolt, then it is not the banquet's fault for offering too little, but mine for wanting too much. I am told to take it or leave it. But if I stay, I must be of good cheer.

It is asking too much.

Although black people have yet to find real, universal belonging in America, there was a time when we belonged to one another. The "black community" is a term of art these days, but once upon a time, it had an address. New York City had One-hundred-twenty-fifth Street. There was U Street in Washington, D.C., Twelfth Avenue in Detroit, Greenwood Avenue in Tulsa, Evans Avenue in Fort Worth, Auburn Avenue in Atlanta, Central Avenue in Los Angeles, Ridge Avenue in Philadelphia, Davis Avenue in Mobile. It was the Five Points District in Denver, the Fillmore District in San Francisco, Deep Ellum in Dallas. Roanoke had Henry Street, Seattle had Jackson Street, Albany had Pearl Street. It was Fulton and Nostrand in Brooklyn. Where I grew up, in Little Rock, Arkansas, it was Ninth Street.

The old walls of segregation were solid and strong then, fortified by law in many locales. Timbers of ignorance and fear gave the wall its height and durability. One side of the wall served as a palisade, designed to protect white privilege from the rest of us who might creep upon it and snatch a piece. On that side, freedom was immense, bordering on boundless.

Black people lived on the other side. On that side, the wall was a fence, a barricade, built to restrain us, to confine us and our dreams and ambitions and, to no small extent, our rage. On that side, freedom was slight and stingy.

In 1954, the United States Supreme Court took a chunk out of the wall by striking down the "separate-but-equal" doctrine of public education. This new hole in the wall poured a beam of hopeful light on American schools, though the beam would be dimmed by white resistance. In my hometown, the all-white Little Rock School Board had already turned subversive, devising a plan of determined dilatoriness in answer to the high court's mandate of "all deliberate speed." The board's idea was to permit desegregation at the high school level initially, and then only by allowing a select group of academically accomplished Negro students into the venerated Little Rock Central High. The plan was to begin in the fall of 1957.

Further, the desegregation of Central High was to proceed only if construction of a second public high school was completed before the school year began. Situated in an all-white, upper-middle-class pocket of the city, Hall High School was to be a refuge for those white students who could not bear going to school with black students, not even the few who eventually enrolled at Central. Thus was the wall regirded.

While the intrepid Little Rock Nine were stepping into danger and into history that perilous fall of 1957, most blacks in the city took comfort in the safety and sameness of the all-Negro world in which they lived. Whatever treachery and uncertainty awaited on the other side of the wall that Jim Crow had built, we felt at ease on our side. What we lacked of life's finery, we had of its necessities in abundance, thanks to the industry and will of black entrepreneurs and good neighbors.

In cities and towns across America, black districts presented an eclectic mix of establishments and lifestyles. There were beauty and barber shops, dry-cleaning establishments, nightclubs, theaters, grocery stores, cafés, billiard halls, mortuaries, boarding houses, insurance companies, doctors, lawyers, dentists, optometrists, and a raft of churches. In a spiritual sense, places like Ninth Street belonged to every Negro in the city and every Negro belonged to them. They were the one place any of us could go and get what we came for without threat or insult. When our mothers needed their curls freshened or our fathers needed their hats blocked or one of us Negro children had an earache that would not respond to warmed sweet oil and our mother's cuddling, the Ninth Streets of America were the destination of recourse.

For all its deprivations, all of its walled-off opportunity, the black side of town, as it was known then, was a cozy place to be. The air was perfumed with possibility, striving, and, best of all, togetherness. Adults were expected to care for all children in their sight, and this duty included the right to discipline us, if necessary. Which is why, on Sunday mornings, even the old women who no longer had little children sat with switches in their laps, just in case somebody's child got out of line and needed a swat. We kids might fume, pout, and mutter up a storm if some woman or man we barely knew scolded us or stung us with the switch, but we would not dare put up a resistance or talk back because the understanding was that grown-ups were in charge. Period. Besides, that same woman or man might just as easily jerk us back from oncoming traffic or shield us from some miscreant. We were content with the double-edged sword of village watch care.

Back then, children did not die in the black community except as a result of the occasional drowning, car accident, or acute illness. Small caskets were rare sights then. When a child died, like the little family friend who was accidentally strangled while playing tether ball in his own yard, the whole community was gripped by grief, sullen and horrified that such a thing could happen. Homicide of and by youths just didn't happen. Naturally, there were questionable characters, young and old. Dangerous people, even. But there was no widespread or stalking fear—not on our Ninth Streets despite their combustible mix of the seedy and the sublime.

In Little Rock, white residential areas fanned out west of Ninth Street. A patch of modest houses formed a gateway to the decidedly upper-crust section of the city, where black people went only to mow someone else's lawn, haul someone else's trash, clean someone else's house, or tend to someone else's children. But the association with Ninth Street was apparently too much for these sentries. They did not want to be identified with the bastion of Negrodom so, to quench the anxiety, the city fathers bowed to white homeowners' request and changed the white portion of the thoroughfare to Maryland Avenue. Thus were the walls reinforced.

As the hub of black social and business life during segregation, the nation's Ninth Streets also provided a captive audience, a headquarters of sorts for the black populace. Whites with something to say or sell to black folks knew where to head first. So did racists when they wanted to send a message. Like the unforgettable horror show that occurred in Little Rock in the spring of 1927.

Until its demise under the foot of urban renewal, Ninth Street bore the scars from that long-ago atrocity and the black residents memorialized it in whispered oral history. A quarter of a century would lapse between the incident and my birth, yet it was still alive enough in the community to reach my ears sometime in my youth. Every time a black Arkansan was verbally or physically attacked, every time a black Arkansan cried police brutality, every time justice turned its back on a black Arkansan, the ghost of the 1927 terror returned.

It had begun when a Mrs. B. E. Stewart and her daughter rushed into downtown Little Rock in their horse-drawn wagon on a fine May morning. Harried and disheveled, Mrs. Stewart was hysterical, telling a gathering crowd that she and her daughter had been accosted by a "colored" pedestrian as they rode into the business district from the town's rural edge. Mrs. Stewart said the man stopped the wagon to ask directions when, suddenly, he jumped into the wagon and demanded whiskey. The *Arkansas Gazette*, reporting the woman's version without benefit of disclaimers or attribution, picked up the story from there:

> *Almost without waiting for an answer, he started beating the two women with an iron bar, the first blow knocking Mrs. Stewart from the wagon. Another blow caught the daughter a glancing blow on the neck and she fell out of the wagon. An approaching automobile frightened the Negro away.*

What happened in the hours following the alleged attack was the stuff of black nightmares and southern legend. Hearing Mrs. Stewart's frightful account, the sheriff collected a posse of sworn deputies and what the newspaper reporter referred to as "volunteers"—ordinary white men who held no official license but who were invited to join in the search for the Stewarts' alleged assailant.

In all probability, the posse comprised many of the same men who, only short weeks before, had appeared at the county jail one night with the intent of seizing a sixteen-year-old black murder suspect. The boy, a handyman at a downtown Presbyterian church, was accused of having killed the pastor's twelve-year-old daughter who had disappeared and whose body was later discovered in the church belfry after days of frantic searching. According to the boy's intimates, he and the girl had secretly conducted a minor romantic fling—sin enough, given the ages involved but, in the hidebound segregated South, also the kind of offense that would get a black man or boy strung from a tree or thrown, hog-tied, into a river or torn in two by some citizen's double-barrel twelve gauge.

The boy had reportedly panicked when the girl protested his advances and threatened to tell her parents. The story goes that he strangled the girl and she collapsed into a lifeless heap. The belfry, he thought, would be a choice hiding place for the body since it was rarely visited by anyone except the church bellringer. Instead, it was that very location that incriminated him, as he was the one who regularly rang the bells.

Word of the boy's arrest spread like brushfire throughout the town. Soon a furious mob appeared at a downtown store, armed with torches, ropes, shotguns, and a plan. The black boy, having killed a preacher's child, would have to die certainly, publicly, and soon. The wave of angry white southern manhood rolled toward the county jail. But when the lynch mob arrived at the sheriff's door on the evening of the arrest, it found an empty cell. The sheriff, having anticipated vigilante action, had sneaked the youth out of the jail and to another facility. Although the young suspect would eventually be tried, convicted, and executed within months of his arrest, the mob that night was left to swallow its bloodthirst and leave, seething and unsatisfied.

So when a breathless woman and her daughter raced into town shortly thereafter with a tale of yet another black predator, the posse organized quickly and set out for the western fringe of the city from whose woods they eventually plucked a thirty-six-year-old man named John Carter.

The tag-along *Arkansas Gazette* reporter said Carter, cornered by the mob, fell to his knees "begging the possemen to spare his life." But, the reporter wrote, onlookers took no mercy.

"Officers attempted to bluff the crowd out of its intention," the newspaper reported, "but they were themselves threatened and the crowd remained firm in its intention. The mob did not seem to want to torture the Negro, but demanded his death."

Terrified, John Carter reportedly confessed that he had accosted the Stewarts but he denied having brandished a weapon against them. It didn't matter. John Carter was hanged from a telephone pole and riddled by rifle fire. The coroner, who happened to be on the scene, declared Carter dead from multiple gunshot wounds and mused that his killers had apparently left the scene.

They killed John Carter four times over that day. After being hanged and shot, Carter's body was tied to the rear bumper of an automobile that then headed directly toward town, trailed by a line of vehicles bearing participants and spectators in Carter's murder. News accounts said the "gruesome parade" made several passes by police headquarters where officers vainly attempted to disband the convoy. The procession then moved, with studied cruelty, toward Ninth Street.

It was midafternoon when the death squad turned onto Ninth, dragging the shredded body of John Carter up and down the avenue over cobblestones and curbsides for more than an hour. Horrified shopkeepers, children, old women, cooks, insurance men, pool hustlers, errand boys, jazz musicians, and ministers watched as the cars made several passes. When the mob of killers grew weary of displaying Carter's mutilated corpse from the car bumper, they unhitched it, dumped it onto the streetcar tracks in front of the Bethel African Methodist Episcopal Church, stripped pews from the church's sanctuary and broke them into kindling, piled the wood onto Carter's body, doused the heap with gasoline and set John Carter's remains on fire.

"During the three hours in which the horde of maniacal men ruled the city, there was an almost constant rattle of small arms in the vicinity of Ninth Street and Broadway," the *Gazette* reported. "The firing was aimless, directed into the air or into the pavement. One Negro was severely beaten and a white boy was shot accidentally through the leg. Except for the sound counsel of one sane man . . . the Negro would have been burned alive on the funeral pyre of John Carter." It took seventy heavily armed National Guardsmen, deployed by the governor, to restore some semblance of order.

The relative security that black residents of Little Rock had enjoyed even while huddled in segregation would never be recouped. Businesses closed for days or weeks or for good following the Carter travesty. Many black families left town or sent their children to live with relatives in the North, fearful that tempers might flare anew and the mob would stage another deadly rampage.

This was not just the story of Little Rock. It was the story of America in the earliest decades of the twentieth century. Yet despite the occasional terrorism visited upon the black districts, they continued to serve as sanctuaries for souls weary of dealing with the suspicious looks, the questions, the insults, and the threats that lurked outside the wall.

But the fear, anger, and confusion that gripped our ancestors, prompting them to spirit their own children away—not for boarding schools or world travel, but for mere survival's sake—are, to some degree, present in the marrow of every black child, especially males. The notion that the lynch mob has merely dispersed rather than disbanded and that it waits only for the opportunity to strike again is assuaged by modern law and sensibility, social activism and the surety of fierce black resistance. Otherwise, there is plenty of reason to suspect that, in many hearts and minds, the mob lurks, maybe not with killing on its mind, but certainly to expel, imprison, and isolate blacks they find disturbing for whatever reason or none at all. That, of course, is murder too—the slow, soft kind that slays the ambition, hope, faith, and trust that fuel the human spirit.

Many Americans would just as soon forget atrocities like the Carter murder of 1927. They contend that such recall is unproductive, perhaps even counterproductive, stirring up a bitterness unfit for current times. But since the past parents the present, the effects of history cannot be ignored or discounted, particularly in the matter of attitude and ideology, both as inheritable as brown eyes or long legs or large ears.

We are therefore not only the product of our own experiences, but the product of our ancestors' experiences. What grandmother and grandfather saw, heard, and felt about black-white relations helped shape mother or father who, in turn, shaped us. In the wake of personal experience and enlightenment, the concepts may change but what our elders taught us and told us will invariably have some bearing on our own beliefs, bolting into our consciences to direct the traffic of our lives.

Naturally then, wariness about people of different races is informed by instinct, by personal experience, by history, and by our own ancestors' experiences, all of which may be sadly misinformed or misconstrued. Nevertheless, travesties like the slaughter of John Carter, however long ago, are refreshed each time we witness a major racial injustice. We know that, in some families, racism is an heirloom.

Even when no particular horror had stamped the memory and reputation of the various avenues, streets, and districts that made up the black community—even when the memory is sweet and the reputation proud—reflection is bound to stir mixed emotions. After all, black neighborhoods had been built by segregation and, for that reason, they were reminders of the differences between us and whites, who were considered superior, if not supreme. All the same, a trove of talent, caring, ambition, industry, determination, faith, genius, and good times flourished inside our racial Siberia. It may have been ringed by tribulation, but the black community was ours—the nearest to home we've ever been.

It was not always called the "inner city." It used to simply be "the city." But that was before throngs of blacks moved into urban centers for jobs, housing, and modern amenities. And before white America packed its bags and bedding and headed for the hills and fields that once were forests or farmland. Whether they moved expressly for schools, for fresh air, or for space is arguable. What is clear, however, is that their leave-taking pulled the financial rug from under many cities when they ripped away their patronage.

Nearly half of all black Americans live in large metropolitan areas, often in areas bearing little or no resemblance to the American Dreamscape. They are, for all practical purposes, denizens of another country, isolated from the opportunity and pleasures—and freedoms!—for which the United States is known. Liquor stores and corner markets selling overpriced merchandise make up the business districts. Dope peddlers and numbers runners are the local "entrepreneurs." In the nation's capital, while one upper-crust neighborhood debated the pros and cons of a drive-through gourmet coffee shop, the residents of the city's poorest ward were keeping their fingers crossed that they might actually get a real grocery store in the neighborhood again. Economically, the so-called inner city is about as plugged in to the nation's economic boom as Bangladesh.

"There are so few decent jobs in most urban ghettos that many people simply give up looking for work," wrote Boston College theology professor David Hollenback in 1999. "This amounts to the institutionalization of despair. When human beings are told repeatedly that they are simply not needed, it takes extraordinary self-confidence to keep trying. Such messages, built into class structures of American life today, lead to the drugs and violence of many American urban centers."

In Pulaski County, Arkansas, where I'm from, authorities have identified forty-nine street gangs, three-fourths of them in Little Rock, the state's capital and largest and most prosperous city. The gang problem got so wild there that cable TV giant HBO chose Little Rock as the focus of a documentary on gang life. The local prosecutor had 966 names of suspected gang members in his database, a number he estimated to represent about one-third of the actual gang population. Mind you, Little Rock is a midsize American city.

Of course, when the establishment neglects youth, implying

that they are irrelevant, unwanted, or disposable, the kids—naturally imbued with energy and imagination—are bound to find other outlets. If there are no established ports in which to channel that energy and imagination, young folks will invent them. They crave association, belonging, and purpose. In a bind—especially a long-lasting one—a bad or dangerous purpose will do.

The ultimate objective is to find self-worth and a reasonable degree of respect that, of course, is their birthright. The arrangement is supposed to be that we commit our resources to their careful upbringing in exchange for the probability that they will be confident and productive, prepared to run the world in an orderly manner and ready to rear the next generation of young.

But the country has reduced black youth to a "problem," inviting chaos and a warped code of ethics and conduct. It should be no wonder that handguns are so popular among deprived children. A barrel in one's face evokes fear that, in lieu of the real thing, can look an awful lot like respect. Maybe a kid can't get our attention or courtesy by just being himself, but he can damn sure command it from the business end of a nine millimeter.

Likewise—in the absence of hope and in the face of such widespread apathy—can we not understand the appeal of mind-altering drugs when the mind is so full of bad memories, bad images, and bad dreams? Not to justify heroin and cocaine use, God forbid; I am simply trying to lay out how societal neglect, white flight, avarice, and apathy have created the monsters of the inner city, overshadowing the legion of people who are somehow maintaining their good names and good spirits even as the country shuts them out.

During his aborted attempt to win the Democratic presidential nomination in 2000, former New Jersey senator Bill Bradley called it straight: "White Americans seem to have ignored the devastation in many American cities. It's almost as if the kids with AIDS, the gang members with guns, the teenagers lost to crack cocaine, the young rape victims whose only self-respect comes from having another child, don't exist for most white Americans."

The most insidious aspect of this racial and economic apartheid is the fall-back plan. Under that scheme, if inner city youth cannot be geographically contained and isolated, or if they do not embrace and adapt to the mainstream culture posthaste, then they may find accommodation in one of the many new jail cells across the nation. (These facilities come courtesy of the same people who often complained about "throwing" money at public schools, but from whom there is no complaint about "throwing" money at prisons.)

The decay and disregard of inner city life are always overbearing, but from time to time, they become unbearable. It happened in Cincinnati, in the spring of 2001, when an unarmed black teenager, nineteen-year-old Timothy Thomas, was shot and killed by police. Three days of rioting followed. Though grief and outrage tore through the black community, Thomas's death only lit the fuse. The bomb had been constructed by choking poverty, unemployment, lack of health care, and inadequate housing—all the precursors of desperation.

It is unreasonable, even cruel, to ask or expect poor black Americans stranded in the decaying and abandoned inner cities to make themselves at home. Home is not meant to be so exacting and hostile.

Chapter 6

Deconstruction

Freedom isn't free," goes a popular refrain. Certainly black Americans know it to be true. The cost of attaining and maintaining freedom is measurable not only in livelihoods and opportunity but in lives and dreams. Still, the prize has always been held worthy of the toll, although it is incontrovertible that freedom should never have been a prize to begin with, but rather the most basic of standard equipment.

When freedom came in the form of the 1964 Civil Rights Act, the sky seemed bluer and the sun brighter than they had ever been for black Americans. The promise of the new frontier whereupon black folks had never freely walked was bewitching. Once we got to that promised land called "Equality," the days of turmoil and trouble were surely numbered. Whether living in the legally segregated South or the de facto segregated North, black Americans were steeped in the faith that desegregation—a procedure—would deliver us to that ideal destination: integration. We could not wait to prove what folly segregation had been. Little did the faithful suspect, however, that there was much more to dismantle than simply the doors that had held us at bay. Fear born of ignorance born of long separation had cast black people as aliens who, in our trek across the uncharted plains of desegregation, would be viewed not as prospectors but as trespassers.

Hence, as we arrived, whites departed. They fled the public schools, the neighborhoods, and, in some instances, entire cities. Racism, that old devil, had not left with Jim Crow, but had merely evolved into a more artful character with more sophisticated tactics and disguises, though just as conniving as ever. Here, we had thought the door was our enemy when, as we sadly discovered, it was just the portal to further troubles, which awaited us on the other side.

The early days of desegregation were trying times. There were swift and notable successes at mainstreaming, usually commemorated by news reports and a persistent buzz of excitement in the black community. The first this, the first that. That barrier broken, this challenge conquered. But, as difficult as it had been for President Lyndon Johnson to get his Civil Rights bill through a cantankerous Congress, passage turned out to be the easy part. Getting people to accept and live with the new order was something else.

We undertook this edgy transition while disconnected from all things familiar. As we set out across the new frontier, eager to stake our claim, we scattered in all directions, only to be stranded on foreign and often hostile terrain. As desired as it had been, desegregation demolished the black community. Ironically, the vital organ that had supported and nurtured us ceased to function when segregation ended. Slowly but surely, the black community—once so vibrant—emptied, dried up, and died. Business owners who had been confined to black districts took their chances with fancy new addresses in newly desegregated commercial zones. More white doctors and lawyers opened their doors to black clientele, taking business away from black professionals who had prospered in the black districts. With the housing market now open—at least on paper—homeowners ventured beyond the old neighborhoods on the black side of town and drifted toward residential areas that had blossomed beyond the now crumbling wall.

Mine was the first black family to move onto Little Rock's West Twenty-first Street in the heart of the city. We became known in certain circles as "blockbusters," a pejorative term for people who upset the homogeny of a neighborhood, be it racial or otherwise. We had barely arrived on the block when FOR SALE signs began sprouting up and down Twenty-first. The resistance was wasting no time.

We children were happily oblivious to the significance of the exodus. We were far too thrilled by our new surroundings, not to mention the big new swing set and playhouse Daddy had put up in the backyard. Those attractions and our fondness for making mud pies kept my sister and me too busy to notice all the packing and hauling that was going on around us.

An expanse of Bermuda grass stretched across the front of our new house. There, my sister and I made a game of running, full blast, across the wide, level lawn to the very edge of the sloping terrace and screeching to a sudden halt just short of a disastrous plunge. Then we'd race back to the front porch, sweaty and breathless, and do it again.

I imagine that's what we were up to the day we spotted a cluster of children on the porch of the house directly across the street. White children. Four or five of them huddled on their stoop, watching my sister and me intently. We didn't speak to one another at that first sighting and maybe not the second or third. But eventually we were overcome by the attraction children naturally feel for one another and thereafter my sister and I would bolt straight away for the front lawn to make contact with the kids across the street.

One day, we stopped merely staring and took a more aggressive tack, performing for one another, showing off our competence at hopscotch and hide-and-seek, showing off what fun we could be— that childish seduction which begs, "Don't you wish you knew me?"

It worked. The little band of children inched into the street. Then crossed it. Then climbed our terrace steps and landed on our front lawn. A friendship began instantly and earnestly. The bunch of us giggled and squealed, reeling off playful propositions with dizzying speed. "Wanna play tag?" "You got any dolls?" "We have a playhouse in the backyard." "Let's play chase."

But in the midst of our revelry that first day, there came a distant voice, loud and angry, beckoning our new friends by name. And one by one, they ran, they flew, out of the swings, out of the playhouse, out of the circle where the dolls were having a tea party, out of the tree one had climbed. Most of all, out of our lives for good. The neighbor kids took a good scolding and swatting that day for having consorted with the little colored girls across the street. They were forbidden to ever do it again.

Afterward, whenever we saw the kids across the street again, my sister and I resorted to the old game, the staring game, and would occasionally reprise our siren dance, but to no avail. They never again came to see us. Our ordinary street had become a great chasm that none of us dared cross again, though the temptation burned in us and, I am sure, in them. Before long, the house across the street was vacant too.

New families—black families—began filling up the deserted houses on our block and our playing days were graced anew. West Twenty-first Street exploded with children of all ages, sizes, and temperaments, albeit of only one race—ours—which, truth be told, was just fine with us. Whites were strangers passed on the street or briefly encountered in the store, but they weren't friends. How could they be in their separate world? Every now and then we'd ask a question about them or make a comment about them, but for the most part, we children were satisfied in our all-black world, unattuned to the inimical purpose behind the balconies and back doors and rear seats to which we were consigned.

Being dissatisfied with the status of things was our parents' province. While they grappled with injustice, we children concentrated on easier things like bicycle races, grade school crushes, junior choir rehearsals, or fat sour pickles from Powell's Grocery Store where our families had accounts. We lived in our partitioned world without question or protest, unaware of the obstacles ahead.

In our blissful ignorance, we peacefully trailed our mothers into stores and offices, taking note of when their soft faces turned to armor in case someone tried to get nasty. In school, we dutifully studied the antics of blue-eyed Dick, Jane, and Sally with no appreciation of the irony of it all. We laughed heartily at *Amos 'n' Andy*, unaware of the demeaning implications. We envied Princess and Kitten on *Father Knows Best.* We passed by theaters, restaurants, and swimming pools without pause, understanding that they were off-limit although we really didn't know why. We did know that asking to go inside would bring either scowls or tears to our parents' faces, which distressed us, so we didn't ask.

For my fifth-grade year, I transferred from my little all-black elementary school to another all-black school newly abandoned by white students. The former tenants had moved to a brand-new school built for them farther out in the city where whites were gathering, having surrendered the inner city to black encroachment. As we moved into the school, we discovered the white tenants had taken all of the playground equipment with them, leaving us with a wide but barren field. Our teachers and parents were demoralized at first, but soon they bought bats, gloves, and balls for us and turned ours into a softball-loving school.

My mother, then a first-grade teacher, often found the slights maddening, such as the time she took her young class to a performance of the *Nutcracker* ballet at a city auditorium. The little ones, being black, had been routinely directed to the upper balcony of the auditorium. There, too small to see over the railing, they had squirmed and bobbed throughout the performance, straining for a peek at the stage. Mama said she had been grateful for the darkness in the concert hall because it allowed her to hide her tears. That's the way grown-ups often dealt with the blows of discrimination in those days—hiding their anger and pain from the children, lest we become afraid, embittered, and hopeless. Still, my mother vowed never to take another class to the auditorium until equal rights and fair play found its footing.

It did not appear to me as an epiphany that the color of a person's skin figured into the dispensation of rights, privilege, justice, and opportunity. Rather, it came as a creeping awareness, a gradual realization that struck me then, as now, as the most ridiculous notion I had ever known. The first time it made my blood boil was in a Woolworth's store where my sister and I, no more than eight and ten years old, had taken our small allowances to make Christmas purchases. Somewhere in the crush of shoppers, Sandra and I were separated. When I found her, she was standing near the lunch counter, swooning over the hot fudge sundae being prepared for a white customer. The big menu board over the griddle priced hot fudge sundaes at forty cents—a sum I could afford but did not offer. Somewhere along the line I had learned that Negroes were not served at the downtown lunch counters, so I made no move. But I will always remember my sister's sweet, young face. And I will always remember the pangs that rippled through me that day as I stood there, helpless, unable to treat Sandra to the simple delight she longed for, on account of her race. I was good and mad that day, finally taking Sandra's hand and leading her away. Neither of us knew the word "discrimination" then, but we sure knew what it felt like.

That was the kind of foolishness the Civil Rights Act was supposed to eradicate—that and more serious stuff. There were significant changes in where we could go and what we could do, but the reception we often received belied the law. In the summer of 1964, I realized it would be a while before we could reap promise from the Promise Land.

My mother had been away for much of the summer, enrolled at the University of Arkansas at Fayetteville, one-hundred-fifty miles north of Little Rock. We were proud of Mama and her impending master's degree in elementary education. But her leave-taking had left a hole at home. We children suffered a terrible pining during her six-week absence even though our summer days were relatively easy and carefree. Daddy, a renaissance man before his time, proved himself to be an able pinch hitter in both the kitchen and at the dressing table where he patiently tied our dress sashes into perfect bows and gathered our hair into neatly pinned pigtails. Still, it wasn't the same.

Ribbons of smooth interstate highway flow between Little Rock and Fayetteville today, but in 1964, the route was a maze of hazardous, two-lane curves through the mountains of northwest Arkansas. Because it was such a hike, Mama had been able to take only one furlough from the U of A, hitching a ride with several other black graduate students who had likewise left families back home in pursuit of higher education and the opportunities it promised.

We weren't sure what time the car bearing our mother would arrive that day, but my sister and brother and I got up early and tried to wait out her arrival at the top of the long front terrace steps. As the sun was setting, Daddy collected us for baths and dinner, hoping, no doubt, to distract us from our anxious wait. Once done with dinner, we begged to resume the vigil. Daddy was a pushover for us. When the car with our mother last arrived, he was with us at the top of the terrace steps.

The brief weekend visit had been rejuvenating. To my everlasting relief, it chased away the terrible fear I harbored that, in my mother's absence, I might forget her face. The sight of her soft, youthful smile and her steady, warm embraces had made a fine antidote for the little girl blues. I cried strenuously when the car came to take her back to Fayetteville, but at least my worst fears had been vanquished.

When graduation day finally came, the elation in our household could hardly be contained. This time, we wouldn't have to wait for someone to bring our mother to us; we were going to fetch her. Daddy made big plans. We would leave for Fayetteville at first light on Saturday morning. Once there, we would go straight to Mama's dormitory and collect her. Commencement exercises were scheduled for late afternoon.

Adding to the excitement, Daddy informed us that we would spend Saturday night at Fayetteville's Holiday Inn, a treat for practically any family in the simpler 1960s. We kids listened as Daddy made the hotel reservations by phone. We were wild with excitement.

I hardly remember any of the long, risky trip along the winding highway that day. My thoughts were not on the farmlands and lakes and river valley we passed, but on the imminent reunion with my mother and the hotel stay, which I had predetermined to be magnificent. In due time, we had Mama, her books and suitcases, and a car full of joy. We headed for the Holiday Inn.

"You all wait here," Daddy said as we drove into the hotel parking lot. "I'll check in and get the key."

The car was overtaken by laughter and kisses and reports about this skinned knee and that lost ball and how Mrs. Byrd's niece and I nearly broke the porch swing from swinging too high. As the sun shone brilliantly upon Fayetteville's rolling hills, life seemed perfect.

But when Daddy returned, our elation sagged and then faded. A sullen expression crept across my mother's face as she studied her husband. Clearly, something was wrong. Daddy said nothing when he got in the car, but grabbed the steering wheel and briefly stared at nothing, it seemed. He shook his head slowly.

"What happened, honey?" my mother asked. The exasperation in her voice said she already knew.

"They said they didn't know I was a Negro when I called to make the reservation," my father answered in all but a whisper. He paused, then jerked the keys out of the ignition.

"Honey, let it go," my mother said. "The children."

Without another word, Daddy put the car in reverse and pulled out of the driveway. Soon, the Holiday Inn faded in the distance. None of us kids asked any questions but tried to distract our parents and recover the merriment. I led my siblings in a silly song, hoping our folks would assume we hadn't caught on to what had just transpired. It was something I learned over the years; that the thing that stings black people the most about discrimination is what it does to their children. What I remember now is how fervently we kids wanted to protect our parents against that self-same sting.

That afternoon, Mama graduated, resplendent in her cap and gown. Among the graduates was the son of Orval Faubus, the Arkansas governor and instigator of the Central High desegregation crisis of seven years before.

That night, my parents slept in the guest room, while my sister and brother and I slept on a soft pallet in the living room of a generous black Fayetteville couple who barely knew us, but who were all too familiar with the circumstances that had necessitated their kind hospitality.

Chapter 7

Schoolhouse Blues

There is a reason some of the first and most significant scores in civil rights were made in the educational arena—a reason that the 1954 *Brown* v. *Topeka Board of Education* Supreme Court ruling is considered the granddaddy of modern black advances. Black people have always revered education as the great equalizer. For us, faith in the powers of education are like biscuits and sorghum—sweet and filling, nourishing and good. We have always understood the power of knowledge. We knew it was why, during slavery, blacks were discouraged from, even punished for, learning to read. We knew it was why our parents and grandparents had risen at the crack of so many dawns and trudged over miles of hill and dusty dale to a one-room shanty in the clearing where black children could learn to read and write and multiply, provided it wasn't harvest time. We knew education was a passport to something better. So when the U.S. Supreme Court ended school segregation with the *Brown* decision, black Americans ripped off the "badge of servitude" that Justice John Marshall decried half a century earlier when his colleagues on the Court affirmed separate-but-equal. In *Plessy* v. *Ferguson* (1896), the Court majority disclaimed Marshall's warning, reasoning that segregation stained black people with inferiority only "if the colored race chooses to put that construction upon it." *Brown* recognized the insolence of that rationale and put the foolishness to rest. The *Brown* decision acknowledged equality of blacks and whites with the promise of access to well-oiled schools to boot. We were on our way home.

We had not anticipated that, as we were running toward a society that had excluded us for so long, that society would start running the other way. At least we had not anticipated how frantic the retreat would be. White resistance to desegregation was fierce. In city after city, white families pulled up stakes and fled to the untamed suburbs, carving new civilizations out of woodlands and cornfields, reconstituting segregation in a sanctuary from the approaching Negroes and their children. Apparently, based on negative presumptions, they were threatened by the prospect of black bodies in their children's schools, and were not willing to find out if the stereotypes were true. In a blink, millions were gone, installed in either private schools or public ones newly built in the fresh fields of white suburbia.

They took away more than their children when they left. The spiritual support, patronage, and the tax base necessary to a school's success were gone too. Though many whites paid lip service to desegregation, their support was, at best, conceptual. In practice, desegregation was anathema. No matter what the new laws proposed, whites resisted the new-fangled racial balance plans and busing and school assignment plans intended to enforce them. Gradually, predominantly white schools became predominantly black schools. The trend continued throughout the final quarter of the twentieth century until, by century's end, racially segregated public schools had been reborn. In June 1999, Harvard researchers Gary Orfield and John T. Yun reported that white students typically attend "overwhelmingly white schools" even in areas with significant ethnic diversity. "In our schools, the color lines of increasing racial and ethnic separation are rising," wrote Orfield and Yun in a report for Harvard's Civil Rights Project. "Our largest city school systems now serve only a tiny minority of white students. . . . Very few have more than one-third whites." Suburban white students in large metropolitan areas attend even less diverse schools. Fewer than 15 percent of their classmates are black and Latino.

If the deserters had removed only their children from the schools and not taken their goodwill with them, we would have far fewer worries. As black children proved from the start, their ability to learn and excel is in no way tied to the proximity of white students. But, as nature abhors a vacuum, affection for public schools was promptly replaced by distrust and dislike once white students evacuated. Whites turned sour on schools with ever-increasing black student populations, and their biases about black virtue, black intelligence, and black ambition were unleashed anew. Today, as ever, white Americans regard black-dominated schools as inherently, definitively, and incurably inferior. Actually, the stigma is so stubborn that it even attaches to schools with a less-than-majority black population. All it takes is a significant black presence for stereotypes to take hold. A 50 percent black population is generally considered the "tipping point," though some experts say white retreat tends to accelerate when black enrollment reaches half that level.

In some cities, public school boards are scrambling to create at least the appearance of equality. For years, the public schools in Montgomery County, Maryland, maintained a stark duality. Whitman High School, with its overwhelmingly white and upper-middle-class student population, was such a commodious and striking edifice that the locals took to calling it "Nordstrom High," after a fancy, upscale department store. Other high schools in the district had predominantly or heavily black and Latino enrollments. Year by year, they deteriorated from overcrowding, wear, tear, and neglect. Occasionally, when the board entertained proposals to send some of the Whitman students to other schools and vice versa, the Whitman parents banded in protest. With their sizeable wealth and political clout, they invariably prevailed. Their special school—their Nordstrom—would not be defiled by interlopers.

The other schools have since been brought up to par with spanking new or substantially remodeled structures. It will be harder to repair the damage done to students' egos and sense of self-worth. By high school, they've usually gotten the message.

The sheer repetition of the inferiority rap chews away at support for public schools. The community pulls back, as evidenced by voters' regular rejection of property tax increases—the local revenue source for many U.S. public schools. Facilities age and decay in the wake of depleted budgets. When equipment fails, it is patched together. Supplies dwindle. Teachers, frustrated by low pay, the dearth of resources, the crumbling and crowded environs, and the worsening reputation of their workplace, grow apprehensive of their charges. Students feel unwanted and burdensome. They are demoralized by this place where their dreams are supposed to flourish but, alas, are in grave danger of withering under the blaze of neglect and repudiation.

Unmercifully, they are not deafened to the outside world's wailing, its defeatist prognostications, its complaints about the "waste" of tax dollars. They hear the objectors. They see them racing away. Running, running, always on the run from schools damaged, first and foremost, by their cruel suppositions. The Harvard researchers Orfield and Yun write:

> *Though we usually think of segregation in racial and ethnic terms, it's important to also realize that the spreading segregation has a strong class component. When African-American and Latino students are segregated into schools where the majority of students are non-white, they are very likely to find themselves in schools where poverty is concentrated. This is of course not the case with segregated white students, whose majority-white schools almost always enroll high proportions of students from the middle class. This is a crucial difference, because concentrated poverty is linked to lower educational achievement. . . . The nation's large program of compensatory education, Title I, has had great difficulty achieving gains in schools where poverty is highly concentrated.*

According to the Harvard study, the average black or Latino student goes to school with twice as many poor classmates than do white students. In "intensely segregated" schools—about 8 percent of all schools—87 percent of the children are poor.

These disgraceful statistics could have been avoided. Desegregation never guaranteed equalized results, but it was supposed to be the guarantor of equal opportunity. The fearful, the ignorant, and the bigoted snuffed out that potential and continue to do so, setting up a flow chart of deprivation. Today's unprepared students will become tomorrow's unprepared parents and their children will have to forge possibility from scratch. Thus goes the sin, in perpetuity.

"We are floating back toward an educational pattern that has never in the nation's history produced equal and successful schools," report the Harvard researchers. "There is no good evidence that it will work now." Orfield and Yun do not blame revisionism or wishful thinking for the revival of segregated schools, but something more invidious. Predominantly black schools, they say flatly, "are of very little personal importance to the white population. Much of our recent school politics turns on various theories of why these schools are inferior and have not responded well to the reforms of the last generation. The core issues of racial and economic segregation are rarely mentioned in those political debates."

Instead of addressing those influences, the public debate centers on that proverbially futile exercise of rearranging the deck chairs on a sinking ship. Charter schools and vouchers are the buzz words in so-called education reform nowadays, and some charter school and voucher programs have been successful. But, as publicly financed ventures, they merely recycle funds. Furthermore, they operate on the pretense that public schools will have to improve now that they've got competition. But that begs the questions: (1) Why should the only schools available to everyone have to compete?, and (2) What are they to compete with, now that their already strapped reserves are being "shared" with other schools?

Proponents of vouchers are quick to note that black parents are roundly in favor of the alternative. Several surveys, including one by the Joint Center for Political and Economic Studies, find black parents are enthusiastic about vouchers. Not coincidentally, the Joint Center survey also found that nearly 23 percent of black parents rate their local public schools as poor, whereas only 10.7 percent of whites feel the same way about their schools. This goes back to Orfield and Yun's work at Harvard and their findings about the kinds of schools most white children attend versus the kinds of schools most black and Latino children attend. For black parents, vouchers fall into the any-port-in-a-storm category. The plan is seriously flawed. But, when you're desperate, you might try anything.

Once Texas governor George W. Bush took office as president of the United States in January 2001, the Republican party rejoiced over the future of the school voucher plan. Bush had championed vouchers during the 2000 presidential race against Democrat Al Gore, then vice president. Bush's plan called for a $1,500 voucher for each school-aged child. But budget considerations and intense philosophical opposition got the plan tabled. A good thing too. Show me a private school that can provide a quality education for $1,500 per student per year and I'll show you a private school in the bridge-selling business.

There is hardly any precedence upon which to base faith in a voucher system. Until we abolish the prejudices against black and brown children and confess that those prejudices depress the children's ability to thrive educationally and otherwise, until we acknowledge how those prejudices crush the public faith in and will for integration, vouchers will simply relocate the problem.

"I have lots of black students in my kids' schools," said the white California mother of one of my journalism colleagues. "They redrew the lines and brought in a large section of low-income housing kids into my children's elementary school. Test scores dropped. These are kids that need help and they get it. But it dumbs down the curriculum and it takes away from the gifted kids." Given those feelings, I don't suppose she's inclined to embrace an influx of voucher-bearing kids.

The woman's grievances are not unlike those of my seat mate on an airplane not long ago. An elderly white woman, she was on her way home from an extended visit with her daughter, son-in-law, and grandchildren. She worried about the grandchildren on account of their education. "They're so bad," she told me, speaking of the schools. "I'm just glad I got my kids up and grown before all the colored children came. They really brought the schools down."

For a moment, I was stunned by the woman's crudeness. Then I realized that, between her aged eyes and my fair complexion, she did not realize I was black—"colored," as she put it. Not wanting to make a scene, but needing to make a point, I responded with what I considered civil indignation.

"You can't believe everything you hear about the schools. There are great kids, mediocre kids, and not-so-good kids in all colors," I said.

"Oh, but the colored kids have ruined our schools," she answered.

That was it.

"If you don't mind," I said tersely, "I'm going to take my colored self to another seat." And I did, without looking back to see what was registering on the woman's face. It was an instructive encounter, however. It helps to know what some folks are saying when they think the coast is clear.

Still, as long as people consider black children "bad news" for the schools, we can forget about them committing their spirits and resources to those schools, whether the institutions are public, charter, private, parochial, or vouchered. As new-style schools proliferate, I expect stricter admission standards, higher tuition rates, and other restrictions designed to discourage enrollment by you-know-who. Call me cynical, but every moment of our past foretells it.

Even in those school districts with large white student populations, outrageous disparities persist. You will likely find a raft of specialized programs and curricula to assuage the tentative white student who, it is feared, is daily tempted to bolt. To attract and retain white students—and to gratify their parents—most school districts have installed "gifted and talented" classes, advanced placement courses, and "magnet" programs for those students whose abilities and interests are deemed better than those of the average pupil. It is important to note that, for the most part, these innovations did not occur until public schools began aggressively recruiting white enrollees. Accordingly, the proportion of white students in gifted, talented, honors, and advanced placement courses is invariably out of sync with their representation in the overall school population.

Demand for elite programs is persistent and intense. The programs are jealously guarded by white patrons. Forty-five years after the landmark *Brown* decision, Sheila Dobbins, the principal of the largely black Kennedy High School in Washington, D.C., found herself embroiled in controversy and under attack for refusing to curtail enrollment in one such program that white parents had designed primarily for their children. Under Dobbins's control, they feared, the program had lost some of its prestige. Never mind that, school-wide, Dobbins had almost tripled the number of advanced placement tests, cut suspension and dropout rates, and added more preparatory courses for the Scholastic Aptitude Test (S.A.T.), the touchstone of college admission. White parents revolted when she refused to cede control of the elite Leadership Training Institute to them—"to restore the autonomy of the Leadership Training Institute to the community which designed and developed it," in the protestors' words. Summarizing the rift, one black parent told the *Washington Post,* "They act like they're the only ones who want a good education for their kids and that we just want our kids to be in sports." Here's how UCLA Professor Amy Stuart Wells explained the conflict to the *Post:* "White liberal parents are torn between supporting diversity and the symbols of the civil rights movement and realizing that getting their kids into prestigious colleges is very competitive." Wells said educators have coined a term for the phenomenon; they call it "diversity at a distance."

And the racial dichotomy doesn't end with prestigious programs. Whereas those courses are overpopulated by white students, remedial, or special education, classes are overrun by blacks. In Montgomery County, Maryland—one of the wealthiest and purportedly one of the most progressive counties in America—

black students comprise 21 percent of the 130,000 public school students but make up 35 percent of those students designated as "emotionally disturbed." Nationwide, 28 percent of all students in special education classes and 34 percent of those in programs for mentally retarded students are black. Further, black children with mental and emotional problems—whether legitimate or misdiagnosed—are likely to be sent to juvenile court and other punitive institutions while their white counterparts usually end up in treatment facilities. Can there be any doubt that the racial double standard is still hale and hearty, in even these latter days?

The fallout from "diversity at a distance" is significant. The gap in achievement scores between white and black students is an appalling consequence of educational duality. Although the rate of high school graduation has reached equilibrium between whites and blacks, black students' academic achievement, when measured by standardized testing, lags considerably. Asian, white, Native-American, and Latino students all outperform black students on the S.A.T. The College Board, manager of the popular test for college-bound students, notes that "minority students are both overrepresented among low performers and underrepresented among top performers." In one national twelfth-grade test, for example, only 17 percent of black students were rated "proficient" in reading compared to 40 percent of the white examinees. The numbers provide only more grist for the inferiority propagandists who often ignore the important conclusion by the College Board's National Task Force on Minority High Achievement: "The Task Force . . . was unable to dismiss the negative effect of pervasive elements of racism on the academic achievement of some minority students."

Those elements include pressure on black students to disprove their presumed incompetence—a maddening and grossly unfair requirement. My second-born child came face-to-face with it at the tender age of eight. Her third-grade class had spent a couple of weeks preparing for a state assessment exam. Wondering why normal classroom activities had given way to the new daily drills, one of the students asked their teacher why the sudden change. The woman explained that the state government required the tests at certain grade levels to determine whether students were progressing on schedule. And, she said, "to see if black kids can do as well as white kids." When my youngster relayed the conversation to me, I was aghast. I had long fretted that white teachers were no more immune to racial stereotyping than anyone else in the society, but my apprehensions usually yielded to faith in the goodness of education and firsthand experience, which I trusted to overpower those biases. I had trusted unwisely in this case.

Might my young daughter have misunderstood? It seemed improbable, considering that she was too guileless and naïve at age eight to play the race card. I suppose it was simple hope that compelled me to check out the story for myself.

The teacher, a pleasant woman, readily confirmed my daughter's version of what had been said about the test's objectives. As I protested and explained how the comments discouraged black students, embarrassed them, and fueled the inferiority myth, she seemed earnestly surprised that a child might take offense. To this day, I am convinced she had no intention of damaging her black students' self-esteem. It had simply never occurred to her how the words cut. The absence of an ulterior motive was consoling. But, accidental injury can be just as painful as that which is intentionally inflicted. The woman, an educator for heaven's sake, should have known better.

I cannot help but wonder how much better off black children would be were the schools equipped with more black teachers, principals, and administrators. The U.S. Education Department says only 8 percent of the country's teachers are black. Not that more black educators is the cure, but it is bound to improve the odds for black students to have instruction and guidance from men and women who are sensitive to the struggle against negative perceptions and the delicate balance required to navigate the color line. At least theoretically, more black teachers would not only be conspicuous role models for black students, but would also afford the children more access to people in power who do not have to attend sensitivity or diversity classes to understand that black children respond to the same stimuli, or lack thereof, have the same basic needs, and are otherwise fundamentally no different from children of any other race.

Another slice of real life to illustrate the point: My oldest child was ready for kindergarten. The family had just relocated to a suburb of Chicago. The school my daughter would attend is a neat, brick structure, with a well-equipped playground and flowering plants lining the walkways. Nearby, big houses sprawl across fields that used to sprout corn. The area is a model of modern suburbia with its glassy malls and smartly carved thoroughfares. And 98 percent of its denizens are white. My child would raise the little school's black population to five. She would be the only black child in her class.

Her teacher was a perky woman who talked incessantly but cheerfully. I was immediately impressed by her enthusiasm, happy that my child's first teacher appeared to be someone who loved her job. Surely this would be a nice start for her long school career. Then, as I turned to leave that first day, the teacher said something that stopped me in my tracks. "This will be so exciting," she said. "I've never had a black student before." What did that mean? Did the teacher think she was stepping onto new terrain? What might she expect to be different about my daughter? I considered the comment a red flag and filed it away as a caution.

Barely a week passed before the flag flew again, more forcefully this time. "Meredith cannot recite her address and phone number," read the note taped to my daughter's dress. "I am concerned because all of the other children in the class are able to do this. Please call me so we can discuss this."

Swallowing my indignation, I phoned the teacher, explaining that, unlike the other five-year-olds in her class, my daughter had only recently moved to the area. In fact, our family had been in town for only two weeks. "If she needs to be able to give her address and phone number, she'll get it," I said, half nastily. "No problem."

It wasn't long before another note appeared. "Concerned" again, the teacher reported that my daughter had been having some difficulty with a particular math problem, and the woman wondered if I could come in to discuss the matter.

As I was to learn the next morning, several children were having trouble grasping the newly introduced math concept, but the teacher was particularly alarmed for my child only. Why? Because, she said, "I know that underprivileged children may need extra help."

I felt steam rising.

74

"Underprivileged?" I asked.

"Well, I know you aren't working and I see that you're living in an apartment."

"I'm not working because I have two little girls to raise and I don't need to work," I said, no longer keeping my anger in check. "My husband is an investment banker. We live in an apartment because we just moved here and our home is under construction."

The woman demurred. I had her on the ropes.

"Ma'am, my daughter is five years old. We moved her three weeks before school started. The child has no friends in this area. She has no history here. She is going to school for the first time. She is learning. How dare you think that she is underprivileged or less intelligent. Where do you get off?"

I withdrew my daughter from the school that very day. But not before I had had some choice words with both the principal and the superintendent whose ears may still be ringing today from the scolding I gave them on behalf of my child and every black child who might ever grace their doors. Soon we moved back to Little Rock, where my daughter went to school and flourished.

"This will be so exciting," the teacher had said. I doubt she ever imagined how exciting it would be. I have often wondered if she ever learned that excitement is not the appropriate response. Black parents want normalcy. They want dedication. They want patience. They want faith and high expectations for their children. No excitement, thank you very much.

I wish there were no more stories to tell on this front, but there are loads. Such as my son's experience in fourth grade when a white classmate called him "nigger," which he reported to his white teacher, only to be sent back to his desk. The principal, though apologetic, offered a lame excuse for the teacher's abdication. "Many of our teachers have not had black students before," he told me. As if racial slurs are offensive only in mixed company.

Ironically and tragically, much of the educational system is clueless about those areas where black children actually are distinctive. Moreover, it refuses to treat differences as circumstantial, not genetic. Expectations are critical to any child's success and, believe it, black children have noticed the innumerable signs that not much good is expected of them. It is in that rotten atmosphere that inadequate schools fester, setting the kids up for failure and thereby lending credence to the myth that they are, by nature, inept. And let me knock down another myth: Black youths have no aversion to academic achievement, despite a now-popular theory that black kids equate good grades with "acting white." Over the years, I've talked with scores of black students about this and can come only to this conclusion: It is an utter lie. Take Ben, who was seventeen when we talked. He was living in subsidized housing and attended a predominantly black and Latino public high school. Ben was an excellent student. "Nobody thinks getting As and Bs and being articulate is just for white kids," he says. "That's not what we mean by 'acting white.' It's those black kids who only hang with white kids, don't have anything to do with the rest of us, get into the preppy thing and want to get as close to white folks and as far away from black folks as they can. That's acting white."

Scholar and author Claude M. Steele has a theory that is far superior to and more plausible than the "acting white" balderdash. "Beyond class, something racial is depressing the academic performance of these students," he says. Steele believes black students have erected a "psychic defense" against institutional racism. He exemplifies the theme through the story of a former student, a young woman who wanted to be a physician.

> *Her recruitment and admission stress her minority status perhaps more strongly than it has been stressed at any other time in her life. She is offered academic and social support services, further implying that she is "at risk."*
>
> *Once on campus, she enters a socially circumscribed world in which blacks—still largely separate from whites—have lower status; this is reinforced by a sidelining of minority material and interests in the curriculum and in university life.*
>
> *She can sense that everywhere in this new world her skin color places her under suspicion of intellectual inferiority. . . . [S]he risks confirming a particular incompetence, at chemistry or a foreign language, for example; but she also risks confirming the racial inferiority she is suspected of—a judgment that can feel as close at hand as a mispronounced word or an ungrammatical sentence. In reaction, usually to some modest setbacks, she withdraws, hiding her troubles from instructors, counselors, even other students.*

Then Steele nails it.

> *Quickly, I believe, a psychic defense takes over. She disidentifies with achievement; she changes her self-conception, her outlook and values, so that achievement is no longer so important to her self-esteem. She may continue to feel pressure to stay in school— from her parents, even from the potential advantages of a college degree. But now she is psychologically insulated from her academic*

life, like a disinterested visitor. Cool, unperturbed. But, like a painkilling drug, disidentification undoes her future as it relieves her vulnerability.

Where Steele portrays the response to black alienation as "psychic defense," my term for it is "psychic protest," but he and I are on the same page. What should alarm us is not that black students *cannot* match white achievement—they can—but that many have stopped trying. They have quit the proving game, having been underestimated, overlooked, or compromised one too many times. They are tired of counting on education to whisk them to better times, having seen parents, aunts, and uncles who gave it their all, played by the rules, followed the yellow brick road, and still ended up denied, suspected, and unfulfilled.

Too, at every turn, the society has signaled them that it is whiteness that wins, whiteness that succeeds, and whiteness that matters. If access and opportunity do not require you to be white, they at least demand an approximation of whiteness. Conformity to Anglo-American conventions may not indemnify nonwhites against discrimination and exclusion, but it sure cranks up the odds of inclusion, whereas those who wear certain "black" hairstyles, use "black" slang, and "dress black" are likely to be evicted. They are negatively judged for their blackness, often punished for it, while constantly being reminded that, if there is any hope for inclusion, they must forfeit their blackness and adopt the great white way. Those who capitulate to the directive are often seen as traitors for having revealed their appreciation for and envy of white culture. That is what Ben meant by "acting white."

"For black students, then, pressure to disidentify with school can come from the already demoralized as well as from racial vulnerability in the setting," writes Steele. By withholding their participation and adherence to white standards, black students are exercising what power they have against the inhospitable forces that surround them. They are refusing to play the game, even to their detriment. The antidote is to steep black children in positive expectations and to treat them accordingly. Dr. Spencer Holland has proved this with his Project 2000, which has turned some of the poorest children in the nation's capital into confident, smart, can-do achievers. First, Holland said, he had to undo the pain. "Trying to get them to concentrate on academics without helping them with the hurt in their hearts is not going to work," he said.

There are far too few Claude Steeles who understand the social and psychological undercurrents tugging at black academic achievement. There are far too few Spencer Hollands who are devoted to undoing the damage to black youths' hearts and minds. In answer to the dilemmas facing black American students, there is scant good news in the offing. Desegregation itself is in danger. Polls show that most white parents think there is sufficient racial amalgamation in the schools and that education already offers equal opportunity. The majority of black parents think not. Unfortunately, the former opinion has an empowered majority behind it, as well as the courts. In their 1999 report on school desegregation, Harvard's Orfield and Yun cite a litany of federal court decisions that have put a stranglehold on school desegregation efforts. In one, a district court ruled that desegregation orders were not permanent and that, if they chose to, school boards could return to the neighborhood school model. Given housing patterns, the ruling amounts to a green light for segregated schools.

With the judicial system in their corner, "many major school districts are in the process of phasing out their desegregation plans," Orfield and Yun reported. They expect more to come. Then there's Head Start, a program that lives up to its name, serving millions of poor four- and five-year-olds. The program has well-documented successes. The generally accepted cost-benefit ratio is three dollars saved for every one dollar spent on the program. Yet Head Start perennially fights for its life when the federal budget is assembled. Critics point to studies showing a "fadeout" of skills once the child has been out of the program for about two years—reason enough, they say, to curtail expenditures. They do not bother to investigate whether the children's collision with low expectations and prejudices has any role in the degradation of skills. *Why* doesn't seem to matter.

In May 2000, a coalition of civil rights groups sued the state of California for allegedly cheating public school students of the bare necessities in education. A lawyer with the Southern California chapter of the American Civil Liberties Union called the schools "the shame of California." Among other failures, the suit cited a lack of good textbooks and lab materials, absence of libraries, shortage of certified teachers and guidance counselors, massive overcrowding, vermin infestations, broken toilets, and crumbling physical plants. According to the plaintiffs, the worst schools were concentrated in minority communities, leading one ACLU official to label the trend "the Mississippification of California's schools."

Notwithstanding the uphill battle for equality in schools, the resilience of the human spirit should not be underestimated. Hope lives on in the little ones, like the young fellow I spotted one day at the awards assembly of an elementary school in a deeply impoverished neighborhood. At the start of the program, the children recited the pledge of allegiance. *One nation under God, indivisible with liberty and justice for all.* Then, without skipping a beat, the kids broke into a rousing rendition of "My Country 'Tis of Thee" as if the song were part of the pledge. I was captivated by one little mottle-faced boy with uncombed hair and worn, faded shirt and slacks. His tennis shoes were ragged. His arms were pocked by scars that looked like the remains of impetigo. Yet his voice soared above the others. The boy threw himself into the song. *Land where my fathers died, land of the pilgrims' pride. From every mountainside, let freedom ring.* I figured the little charmer to be about five or six years old. Too young to have figured out his sad odds. Too young to know how his fathers died or what all the pilgrims' pride entailed. Too young to know how hollow the ring of freedom is in some quarters. Most of all, too young for his eyes to have lost their sparkle of hope and possibility. That was years ago. I wonder if the little fellow's eyes still shine as brightly. I pray there is some sparkle left.

In the education reform arena, some educators, many black parents, and most black students will tell you that what they need most is a sense that they are wanted, the foregone conclusion that they are competent, positive expectations, buildings that are comfortable, safe and well equipped, teachers and administrators who actually like them, and a climate of acceptance. They only want to feel like a place is being made for them. A good place. A place that feels like home.

Chapter 8

Take a Number

In the waning weeks of my eighth-grade year at Little Rock's now-defunct West Side Junior High, I received an unexpected summons to the principal's office. He had a proposition for me: Sign up for cheerleading tryouts and I would be assured a slot on next year's squad. The principal explained that the school, with a growing black population, wanted to have some "Negro" cheerleaders. I was pleased by the outreach effort, having been well aware of unhappy rumblings within the student body and even some parents and teachers about the incongruity of largely black sports teams and all-white cheerleading teams. I was honored that the principal had tapped me to break the color barrier.

But I was not their girl. Even in junior high school, cheerleading was tough and demanding. To do it well, I would need to execute high leaps, flips, and, hardest of all, splits—that daredevil defiance of physiology that turns a body into an inverted "T." As a member of the school tennis team—and being only thirteen—I was healthy, fit, and had normal agility. But I could not do splits to save my life. Nor was I especially the cheerleading type. I was not much of a joiner or conformist, nor was I known for my perkiness, as most cheerleaders were. All things considered and flattery aside, I knew I would make a lousy cheerleader. I explained all this to the principal and gratefully declined his offer.

He tried to persuade me otherwise, assuring me that, splits or no splits, my selection was a done deal. It would be good for school spirit, he said. No doubt. Black students yearned for more inclusion in the school that, at the time, was in only about its fourth year of desegregation. Although there had been no violent outbreaks at West Side, racial tensions wafted through the halls and classrooms like a vapor. All of us, black and white alike, were newcomers to desegregation, having just left the one-race havens of our elementary schools a mere year or two or three before. It was also a new experience for most of the teachers, and it showed in impolitic ways. When the girls' chorus performed poorly, the music teacher would snipe, "You nigra girls know you can sing louder than that." Another teacher separated black and white students in his class because "I know you all aren't comfortable with each other yet." The boys' dean, a stern and seemingly humorless man with heavy black shoes and a voice like gravel, marched the corridors, looking for trouble. He betrayed a seething suspicion of black students. The slightest misstep by any one of us—like being in the hallway without a pass— brought swift and inordinately severe punishment.

Consequently, every achievement by a black student was savored as a victory for the race, another step up and forward, another advance toward equal stature for us all. The first black cheerleader, like the first black football captain and the first black student body officer, would automatically become an icon. Luckily, I was able to think past the early gratification that would come with the post and saw, instead, the humiliation I would incur when, on the sidelines of the courts and fields of play, my ineptitude would surely be exposed. How long would my classmates feel good about their first black cheerleader if she could not perform at least as well as the others? And what would it bode for the future of black cheerleaders, given society's inclination for judging the qualifications of an entire ethnic group on the success or failure of a single actor? I turned the job down adamantly the second time, and that was the end of that. I think the principal found me shortsighted and impudent. He must have been relieved when another black girl agreed to join the cheerleading squad. She did us proud too, with her perfect cartwheels, high-flying Russians, athletic Herkies and, yes, splits. She was one of the team's best.

Well meaning as he may have been, the principal apparently had not recognized that, under the circumstances, his proposal to me was not a bow to affirmative action but to its deceitful cousin, tokenism—a word I did not know at the time but whose essence I understood instinctively. Tokenism is a corruption of affirmative action. At its root is the assumption that the term "qualified blacks" is oxymoronic. Either that, or the affirmative actors do not take their mission seriously, exhibiting no enthusiasm for finding people who may look different but can produce the same. For my principal's purposes, my blackness alone was qualification enough. But not for me. West Side did not need a token black cheerleader, but a capable cheerleader who was black. It might have surprised him how little it took to unearth her.

That long-ago lesson has yet to be incorporated into America's great affirmative action debate. Most arguments are hinged on the fairness of racial preferences, quotas, and set-asides that—in the absence of heartfelt commitment to equal opportunity—are our most effective tools. The genuine article rewards qualified, deserving people with the opportunity to prove themselves and to enjoy the payoff from their accomplishment. Real affirmative action has spread the wealth of higher education, employment, and business contracts to men, women, boys, and girls who would have otherwise been overlooked, ignored, or purposefully excluded. Done right, affirmative action does not reward the incompetent or undeserving for the sake of diversity. That would be tokenism and no self-respecting person abides it.

Sadly, too many employers, admissions officers, and contractors are of the Any Black (or Latino or Woman, etc.) Will Do School, filling their slots indiscriminately with people who may not be adequately equipped, then yelping about the unfairness of quotas, set-asides, and racial preferences if and when those people fail. This underhandedness fans the antiaffirmative action flames and feeds the very stereotypes that belie black ability and make affirmative action policies necessary in the first place. When hunting the villains of the affirmative action backlash, follow the trail of tokenism.

Were it not so offensive and absurd, the alleged "stigma" of affirmative action would be a hilarity. According to those who are purveying this notion, beneficiaries of affirmative action are automatically sized up as closet underachievers, the recipients of a favor we neither deserve nor are prepared to exploit. In other words, it cannot be that we actually measure up. Our mere arrival is viewed suspiciously by whites who doubt that we could have gotten the positions without intervention by a policy that demands inclusion and outreach.

Well, they are right about one thing. Many of us wouldn't have gotten in without affirmative action. Without it, power-holders might not have even glanced at us, let alone extended a job, a membership, an enrollment form, or a contract. On that front, we have no argument with naysayers. They are right that, in many instances, affirmative action ushered us to the door. But that is a further indictment of white hubris, not a testament to black incompetence—an irony that escapes the critics.

A contemporary television commercial provides a good analogy. Recounting her day, a woman tells her husband that she visited friends at their new home. Great, says the husband. Not so great, says the wife. The friends' house is nicer and it cost less, she reports. Moans the husband, "I didn't even know those houses were there."

So goes the crux of the affirmative action effort: to remind us that there are other "houses" out there—people who fit the bill and will fill the role appreciably, if only we look around. The histories of both Africa and the West provide ample evidence of the timeless talents of black people. You can be sure that black aptitude and ambition were not born with the advent of affirmative action programs in 1970. It was not then that the black population began to be composed of people capable of running businesses, of mastering higher education, of doing service to civic and recreational clubs, of building bridges or buildings, of governing. My father, for one, was a brilliant man who quoted the classics thoroughly and in context, who wrote poetry and sermons, whose mind for math was astounding, whose work ethic was entrenched, whose honesty and dependability were impeccable. Until he went to college on a shoe-string in 1946, no one in his family of nine had had any viable hopes of education beyond high school. His was a prima facie accomplishment. Yet, even after he graduated summa cum laude with a business degree, he started and remained for many years in the mailroom of a large insurance company, the only noncustodial black employee, though only half a rung higher. When he died in 1986, Daddy was the company's longest-tenured employee, with thirty-six years under his belt. By then he was in management, with a private office, an executive assistant, and the coveted title of "vice president." He owed that to his own indefatigable dedication, a whopping dose of patience, indubitable talent, solid faith, and, no doubt, the modern sensibilities born of affirmative action. I have no doubt that had he been white or lived a generation later, a man of his caliber would have been the company's top man.

There is no telling how many great leaders and doers were by-passed before affirmative action forced America to admit that it had given the talent pool short shrift. It didn't even know—or believe—those houses were there. That is what affirmative action is for. It broadens the field to include those who are ready, willing, and able but who, whether at the hand of ignorance or arrogance, were left out of the mix. Applied affirmative action and individual competence are not mutually exclusive, no matter how often and energetically detractors reiterate the lie. Rather, they are a power couple.

Even some black conservatives rise to the occasion in defense of affirmative action. Glenn C. Loury, an economics professor at Boston University and a prominent black conservative commentator, decries the stigma attached to affirmative action beneficiaries. In 1997, Loury responded to Stephan and Abigail Thernstrom's book, *America in Black and White: One Nation, Indivisible* (Simon and Schuster, 1997), to which Loury took notable offense. In their book, the Thernstroms, white educators and researchers, attributed ongoing racial tensions and disparities to angry black people who focus on the bad news rather than on what progress has been made and on what we might do to make further strides. According to the authors, black Americans are self-absorbed and prone to cry racism—or "play the race card"—when things go badly. The Thernstroms call it "the figment of the pigment."

Loury, who has his own qualms with affirmative action, took on the Thernstroms' pithy but erring assessment in full throat. "Perhaps I could put it this way," he wrote in *Atlantic Monthly:* "It's not the *figment of the pigment* but the *enigma of the stigma* that underlies our drama in black and white" [emphasis his].

Loury goes on:

> *That a successful middle-class black man in this country cannot buy or sell a home, raise and educate his children, or pursue his life's work without having constantly, and in innumerable ways, to deal with the stigma of race surely has something to do with the survival in that man's mind of a fealty to "his people." If you want him to abandon the figment of the pigment, why not lend a hand at dispelling the enigma of the stigma?*

Say it loud, my brother.

Predictably, the Thernstroms try to mask their prejudice by publicly endorsing black people who meet their approval. The authors chose, as their exemplar, retired Army general Colin Powell, a man of sterling repute, the first black U.S. secretary of state and, before that, the first black American to chair the joint chiefs of staff. Powell was such a standout and so wildly popular, that, in 1996, mainstream organizations and political operatives made concerted efforts to lure him into the presidential race as a Republican candidate. Bombarded by appeals to run, Powell seriously considered it for months. The country writhed in anticipation and debated the pros and cons of a Powell candidacy. Ultimately, however, the general's reservations prevailed. To the chagrin of many, Powell announced that he would not be a presidential candidate in 1996, in part because of his wife's deep concerns that her husband would become a particularly tempting target for assassins. "There are a lot of crazy people out there," said Alma Powell.

Despite Powell's misgivings about a White House bid, the Thernstroms and other social commentators of the day chose to think of him as all but oblivious to his race and, for that, they applauded him. Powell, however, disputes the impression. In fact, he has made it clear that he is keenly aware of his race, the unique dynamics of being black in America, and the role affirmative action played in his oft-lauded achievements. He is the offspring of aptitude and affirmative action and, to his credit, remains a defender of the policy. In the *Atlantic Monthly* essay, Loury scolded the Thernstroms for fostering misimpressions about Powell vis-à-vis the race issue. "He knows, and freely says, that but for being black he would never have risen to his position, and having so risen, would never have commanded the political interest that he did," Loury writes, to correct the record. "[H]is life story is no brief for racelessness— quite the contrary. Indeed, just about every effective strategy of which I am aware that is being carried out in poor black communities to combat the scourges of violence, low academic achievement, and family instability builds positively on the kind of ethnic consciousness that Powell's biography exemplifies."

Once again, representatives of the obstensibly intellectual class have besmirched a program whose success is intuitively, experientially, and statistically supported. (Julien Benda warned us all of the "treason of the intellectuals" decades ago, but the treachery continues. Smart thinkers still lend their intellectual weight to the "compact impassioned mass," emboldening them in their unrighteousness.)

Common sense tells us that resolute efforts to recruit a particular group to something they would be attracted to in the first place will most likely result in increased ranks. Millions, like Colin Powell, can personally attest to the utility of affirmative action. And for those who are not swayed by either common sense or actual experience, there are abundant studies and surveys that underline the salience of affirmative action. In practically every professional field, the numbers of black Americans have increased considerably, boosting them and their families into the middle class or beyond, whence they may bestow privilege and possibility upon their children as insurance for continuing success. Affirmative action has rewarded blacks for their initiative. For example, thanks to set-asides, minority-owned financial institutions now handle a share of the federal government's bank accounts. A 1969 executive order by President Richard Nixon established the program, but it was largely ignored until recently, when the government made deposits in more than one hundred minority-owned banks and savings and loans.

In 1978, only 0.5 percent of all broadcast license holders were black. Today, black broadcasters own about 3 percent of the market—because they were ready for business and the Federal Communications Commission made a commitment to include them.

Then there's the U.S. military, generally recognized as the beau ideal of affirmative action. Black service in defense of America precedes independence. Five thousand blacks served in the Revolutionary War. Black regiments, like the legendary Massachusetts 54th, were valorous in the Civil War. Blacks answered liberty's call in both world wars with storied courage. We were there in Korea, in Vietnam, in the Persian Gulf. Black men and women are front and center every time America calls them to arms. Yet it was not until July 1948 that segregation in the U.S. armed services was abolished by way of President Harry Truman's Executive Order 9981 to instill "equality of treatment and opportunity for all persons in the armed services without regard to race, color, religion, or national origin." In due course, desegregation gave way to something grander, namely the advancement of nonwhite servicemen and -women. In 1949, fewer than 1 percent of all military officers were black. Today, nearly 8 percent of the officer corps is black. As recently as 25 years ago, only 5 percent of active duty officers were black. Now, 13 percent of that group is black. Again, the marriage of individual readiness and institutional affirmative action is responsible for this measurable progress.

Regardless of these successes, affirmative action is under intense assault. Acting in tandem, the dishonest affirmative action stigma and cries of "reverse discrimination" have drawn quite a crowd. Anti-affirmative action fever has gripped much of the country, led by California, the nation's foremost laboratory of racial diversity. In

1996, more than half of the Golden State's voters approved Proposition 209, outlawing affirmative action in hiring, contracting, and education in state agencies and schools. The proposition's champion was a Sacramento management consultant named Ward Connerly, a black man, at least in appearance. The state's conservative governor had given Connerly a plum post on the University of California Board of Regents and it is there that the governor's servant tested and fine-tuned his animosity toward a policy that had, in all probability, figured prominently in his own good fortune. After the Board of Regents expelled affirmative action from the university's policy handbook, Connerly set out on a statewide campaign. The year after Proposition 209 passed, black and Latino enrollment plummeted at the University of California's prestigious Berkeley and Los Angeles campuses. Didn't bother Connerly. He was more concerned that the spirit of 209 would be subverted by stealth. "You know that Jamal Washington is likely to be an African-American student," Connerly said after 209 passed. "You know that Pablo Gonzales is going to be a Latino. . . . Having the names on the forms would be an invitation . . . to consciously or subconsciously take race into account."

Despite his peculiar concern that affirmative action supporters would use applicants' names as ethnic clues and then admit blacks and Latinos preferentially, not even the wary, wily Connerly could figure out a way to validate applications without the names of the applicants. In that, at least, he was foiled.

But the passage of 209 did not sate Connerly's apparent appetite for social disruption. Bolstered by newfound fame and a winning proposition, Connerly took his minstrel show on the road. Soon, he was in Washington state, where local rumblings against affirmative action were catching on. Never mind that no ethnic minority group in the state composed more than 6 percent of the population; or that at the University of Washington blacks accounted for only about 1,100 of 37,000 undergraduates, 3 of 166 law school students, and 5 of 176 medical students.

Even in the face of such minuscule percentages, racial paranoia thrived and Connerly pounced on it. He labeled equalization policies as anti-, even counterdemocratic, soaked up the publicity, and helped the state of Washington eradicate affirmative action via Initiative 200, which passed in 1998 with 58 percent of the vote.

Connerly next popped up in Florida, another widely diverse state, and tried to bully Floridians into a showdown. Governor Jeb Bush, young and Republican, was originally a devotee of the Connerly plan. But, fearful that a ballot initiative would produce a high turnout of black voters in the 2000 presidential elections, thereby endangering the proposal and candidates who supported it, Bush opted for a bit of legerdemain known as "One Florida." It would end set-asides and priority treatment for minorities and women in school admissions and the awarding of state contracts, while guaranteeing that the top 20 percent of each high school class would be admitted to a state university—a plan very much like the one Jeb's older brother, then Texas governor George W. Bush, had in mind for the Lone Star State. The elder Bush called his disingenuous plan "affirmative access."

Although Connerly and Jeb Bush were on the same antiaffirmative action page, the Florida governor wanted to avoid the political minefield a referendum on the issue would ensure. Still, he couldn't sidestep the explosives altogether. Black legislators and well-organized students from the historically black Florida A&M

an ideology as much as a program, it has proven impervious to overwhelming evidence that it is counterproductive. It legitimizes negative stigmas and panders to the darker instincts of racial animosity.

What, pray tell, would be the brighter instincts of racial animosity?

Fed up to here with such fraudulence, I am inclined to answer Zelnick in much less civil terms than those used by the erudite Paul M. Gaston, professor emeritus of history at the University of Virginia. Gaston is repulsed by the latest wave of affirmative action antagonists with their stigma-slinging, inferiority-preaching, reverse discrimination–wielding alarms, saddened by their "Orwellian newspeak" and wistful about the bygone activists who beheld affirmative action optimistically.

In contrast to Zelnick's ugly pictorial, Gaston portrays affirmative action in education thusly: "A broad effort to identify potential black applicants and to encourage them to apply for admission, often in the face of institutional and emotional barriers." The policy at his beloved University of Virginia, Gaston explained in a 1999 essay, was informed by higher values.

These include the belief that black people, not individually but as a race, are not genetically inferior to white people. Universities share a national obligation to acknowledge and use their resources to help overcome the effects of historic racial discrimination. Virginia's obligation is peculiarly enhanced by its long history of slavery, segregation, and the denial of education to Afro-Virginians; the effects of historic racial discrimination are far from having been eliminated in social institutions and individual assumptions; abolition of affirmative action would be a major setback for the university's effort to overcome the effects of historic racial discrimination; affirmative action neither excludes nor favors any individual solely on the basis of race; affirmative action is a positive, not a negative, action.

And Gaston's final touch: "It harmonizes with and is essential to the University's overall mission to produce the best educated, most creative, responsible, and public-spirited citizenry possible."

Now that is the thing. At worst, authentic affirmative action leaves someone out—someone who may have wanted the slot and been as qualified for it as the next guy. Most of us have known that lousy feeling at least once in our lives. But it's not as if the privilege is squandered. It goes to another someone who wants it and is qualified for it. Another someone who can parlay the opportunity into personal progress and then multiply it. Another someone who will feed his or her family, educate them, house and clothe them, and set them on the course of prosperity. Another someone who will pay taxes and vote and keep his lawn trim and stand for what is right. Let the loser yell "foul" if he must, but let it be because he is so downcast and dejected over having lost so desirable and deserved a place at the table. Do not let it be because the victor is black or Latino or Native American or female. They are all Americans, for God's sake. Their triumph should hurt no worse than any other's.

Yet, apparently it does. When two or more whites are in competition, the winner is deemed either better qualified than the rest or his advantage is said to be a function of nepotism, cronyism, or favoritism. The spurned may sulk, even sue, but the grudge can be significantly less when compared to the animosity aroused by black preference over white. And when a white wins the spot over a black candidate, well, *que será*.

Seldom in modern times has white preference been so profoundly displayed as in Piscataway, New Jersey, where, in the late 1980s, the school board had a quandary. Because of budget shortfalls, it had to eliminate a teaching post in the high school's business education department. Based on seniority, the choice came down to two teachers: Debra Williams and Sharon Taxman. One of them would have to go, but which?

When school officials pored over the women's files looking for distinctions that might help them decide who to let go, they found veritable twins. The women had equal qualifications. Their performance ratings were identical. They had even been hired the same day. Indeed, the dissection of the teachers' records turned up only one difference: race. Williams was black. Taxman was white.

Since the teachers had every important determinant in common, the school board had to find another factor on which to base their decision. Once they noted that the business education department had no black teachers, that was it. Both Williams and Taxman were good teachers, the board decided, but Williams could bring much-needed diversity to the staff. Taxman was dismissed. She sued, claiming discrimination. To its shame, the Civil Rights Division of the senior George Bush's Justice Department joined the case on Taxman's side. Later, when Bill Clinton became president, the Justice Department reversed itself and took the school board's side. Eventually the case was settled out of court, in part because the National Association for the Advancement of Colored People detected the U.S. Supreme Court was not feeling sympathetic toward the black plaintiffs. This, after all, was as the antiaffirmative action mood was coming to a head in the wake of California Proposition 209.

Pray tell, how did the Piscataway School Board discriminate against Taxman? On what possible pretense could she even allege it? Sure, she may have been rightfully upset about getting the boot, but how could she charge discrimination given the unusually level playing field? Or, could it be that Williams's race was, in Taxman's view, a demerit—the great, hard-sought *unequalizer*? Just how solid is white entitlement?

Now let us entertain a contrary notion, one that might even be considered radical given our skittishness about race. This snap-to-it comes courtesy of a 1977 essay in the *Atlantic Monthly* by McGeorge Bundy, former head of the Ford Foundation and President John F. Kennedy's national security adviser:

> *Now we are right at the heart of it. Is race itself permissibly such another thing to look at? If I am a qualified black . . . may not my blackness perhaps make me more qualified? Have I had something extra to go through? If I score 550 where a middle-class white scores 650, have I shown as much or more of what is so critical to success in learning—a determination to learn? Can I bring a different and needed perspective? Is there a special need for people like me in courts and hospitals and on college faculties? May the profession itself be better if more people of my race are in it? Can my presence and participation as a student enlarge the educational experience of others? Does the whole society somehow have a need for me in this profession that it simply does not have, today, for one more white? If the answer to these questions, or some of them, is yes, are*

*not my qualifications by that much improved, and improved pre-
cisely by my blackness? If so, at some point it becomes right that I
should be admitted; I am not "less qualified" when all things are
considered.*

Bundy wrote that in reaction to the infamous Allan Bakke case.
Bakke was a white applicant to the University of California at
Davis School of Medicine. He claimed he was denied admission
because sixteen out of one hundred slots in each freshman class
were reserved for nonwhite students. The policy had been established by the Board of Regents (obviously before Ward Connerly
got his affirmative action appointment). After winding through the
lower courts, the Bakke case arrived in the U.S. Supreme Court,
which upheld race-based admissions standards, provided they contained no numerical quotas.

Quota hysteria has been rife ever since. In spite of his valiant
effort, Bundy did not quell it. Neither did Derek Bok, president
emeritus at Harvard, and William G. Bowen, president of the Andrew Mellon Foundation. Their massive study of the effects of affirmative action in the twenty years after Bakke rendered the
policy's accomplishments shatterproof. In particular, Bok and
Bowen tracked 700 black students who had been admitted to elite,
majority-white schools in 1976 under affirmative action. In the lot,
researchers found 225 holders of professional degrees or doctorates,
125 business executives, 70 medical doctors, and 60 lawyers. Average earnings? More than $70,000 a year.

Bok and Bowen do not question the impact of affirmative action; they know it has been resoundingly positive, especially at the
elite schools where the policy is most controversial because of the

intense competition for admissions. Black college enrollments increased 61.3 percent between 1986 and 1996. College drop-out rates among black students at elite schools were less than half those of black students at less prestigious institutions. Success breeds success, you might say. High expectations are self-fulfilling. Opportunity is a way-maker.

Affirmative action's foes are hearing none of that. To Empower America's Bennett, the policy is a rogue that "diverted attention away from the most pressing problems plaguing black America— bad schools, violent crime, an out-of-wedlock birth rate above 70 percent." Notably, Bennett does not concern himself with how the *denial* of equal opportunity has eaten away at black America's well-being, leaving so many in desperate straits and so susceptible to bad schools, violent crime, and out-of-wedlock births. What balkanizes us, to use Bennett's term, is not affirmative action but the persistent discrimination that sorts the haves from the have nots.

There are certainly affirmative action opponents more strident than Bennett. One is M. Lester O'Shea, author of *A Cure Worse Than the Disease: Fighting Discrimination Through Government Control* (Hallberg Publishing, 1999). Interestingly, the book's foreword was written by the black self-styled intellectual Walter E. Williams, who quite possibly owed his chairmanship of the George Mason University economics department to affirmative action. Yet Williams endorsed O'Shea's thinking, which goes like this:

> *Human nature being what it is, the temptation must be very strong for a Negro to attribute career disappointments to racism rather than to his own deficiencies, particularly if he has grown up with a similar explanation for difficulties in school in a milieu where it*

was taken for granted that all the problems of his race were the white man's doing.

O'Shea, who describes himself as an economist, lawyer, and investment banker, posits a curious theory about black intelligence. It may not be that it's substandard, says O'Shea, only that it has been clouded by a sense of victimhood—so much so that the black American mind has undergone a kind of psychological mutation. To wit: "Perhaps the juxtaposition of slavery with previous backwardness has somehow produced a defeatist attitude toward problem-solving so that underlying equality of intelligence is unable to make itself known through IQ tests and other indications."

O'Shea detests affirmative action as government policy because it embraces an entire group when, as he puts it, there is no common grievance and, therefore, no legitimate class action.

"There is no universal 'black experience,'" he writes. "With Negroes as with everyone else, individuals' experiences are infinitely varied. A Negro may be the child of a Mississippi farm laborer, a Chicago millionaire, a Washington bureaucrat, a Los Angeles teacher, a New York musician, or a San Francisco welfare mother. There is no special expertise in familiarity with discrimination."

What can we say but, Father, forgive him.

The good intentions of affirmative action notwithstanding, equal opportunity is still, for many people of color, nothing more than a slogan, a disclaimer, a sign on the door. Turn to the same studies that document our progress and you will see how thin a threat to the status quo affirmative action really is. In a half-decade of studies, the federally created Glass Ceiling Commission found that blacks, Latinos, and Asians "moved tenaciously toward the top of the corporate ladder."

But, tenacity had its limits. Even now, whites overwhelm the executive suites and washrooms of the nation's major corporations—to the tune of 97 percent. Black membership on corporate boards of directors is a measly 2.5 percent. Black professional men earn 21 percent less than white men with the same education level and experience; black women make 40 percent less than equally qualified and experienced white women.

Black farmers, designated as "socially disadvantaged" by the United States Department of Agriculture, have all but vanished despite special loan programs that were set aside for them. According to a successful class action lawsuit brought by black farmers against the USDA, they were systematically denied loans, subjected to extraordinary interest rates or other unusual conditions for the loans, or otherwise left to languish, unrelieved and unaided by the setaside program. Because of their "disadvantaged" status, black farmers also have first right of refusal to land seized by the USDA upon default. But in 1994—a good year for such sales—only 53 of the 1,120 farms sold went to blacks.

Not even the proud U.S. military can claim bragging rights. A startling survey by the Department of Defense in late 1999 revealed a troubling divide between black and white morale in the armed services. Even as Defense Secretary William Cohen decreed the military services "second to no other institution in providing equal opportunity for all members," 19 percent of black respondents believed they had received unfavorable evaluations because of their race. The percentage of whites making the same claim was 4 percent. Most blacks reported some kind of racial harassment or offense during their service years. Some military institutions are less equal than others. One-third of the 7,700 members of the Virginia Army National Guard are minorities. But only one-tenth of the Guard's officers are black and none of them is a general. Still, the adjutant general insists the Guard is committed to equal opportunity, "no ands, ifs or buts about it."

Lately, the federal courts have gone on a binge of reversals, paring down affirmative action programs until they are of little use. In 1996, the U.S. Supreme Court declined to hear *Hopwood* v. *State of Texas,* allowing the lower court to prevail in its ruling that affirmative action programs at state-run colleges in Texas, Louisiana, and Mississippi—states where race relations are often testy—were unconstitutional. In 1999, the justices let stand another lower court ruling that struck down the Dallas fire department's program for promoting blacks, Latinos, and women.

A federal appeals court abolished the race-based admissions policy at Boston Latin, the nation's first public school, which selected half of its students on entrance exams and took race into account for the other half. When the court made its decision, Boston Latin was 51 percent white, 21 percent Asian, 19 percent black, and 9 percent Latino. Affirmative action at the University of Georgia was wiped out by a federal judge who denounced the "stigmatizing, polarizing costs imposed by racial classifications."

Subversive tactics abound in the business world. The number of black broadcast licensees may be growing, but owners complain that advertisers frequently demand cut-rate deals or refuse altogether to do business with black-owned stations on the grounds that black audiences are not reliable customers.

At QVC, a home-shopping network, black and Latino show

hosts filed a one-hundred-million-dollar discrimination suit claiming, among other things, that they are relegated to late night shifts.

In Contra Costa, California, black bus drivers filed a discrimination suit, alleging an atmosphere of racism that includes the routine use of racial slurs and the denial of promotions.

Rodney Demery, the first black police officer in Beaver Falls, Pennsylvania, and later the town's first black police chief, reports being harassed by the use of Ku Klux Klan symbols and racial epithets, and that city officials called him a drug dealer. When he suspended an officer for refusing to come to work, the town council reinstated the officer. "I'm at the point where I'm tired of going to work, worried about what they're saying about me," Demery told the *Pittsburgh Post Gazette* in 1999. He quit soon afterward.

Two dozen current and former Amtrak employees accused the rail service of discrimination by failing to provide equal training opportunities to blacks, illegitimately disqualifying black employees for job openings, and otherwise maintaining a racially hostile environment.

The United States Marshals and the U.S. Secret Service have both been hit with serious racial discrimination claims by black professionals.

In the entertainment industry, where progressivism and liberalism are flaunted, the dearth of blacks both in front of and behind the cameras bespeaks rank hypocrisy. Until the NAACP embarrassed show business by exposing its lousy record of diversity, black artists accounted for fewer than 10 percent of all characters in TV sitcoms and dramas on the ABC, CBS, NBC, and Fox television networks, although the black presence had been as high as 17 percent at one time. But black viewership was among the country's highest. According to the Center for Media and Public Affairs, blacks watch 40 percent more TV than whites.

A rare exception to white-dominated programming was a medical drama launched in early 2000 titled *City of Angels*. It featured not only a predominantly black cast, but, for the first time in studio history, a largely black cast of writers and directors. Although the show's principals yearned to be judged on the quality of their work, several black actors and writers acknowledged feeling performance pressure for the sake of the black race. Other studio executives seemed to be waiting on *City of Angels* to rise or fall before undertaking similar projects. Satisfying black viewers was, apparently, a much less decisive factor. Blair Underwood, one of the drama's stars, told *USA Today* that until the NAACP stepped in, the prevailing sentiment in Hollywood was "we've done enough for, quote, 'those people.' "

So, how do the critics get away with their disdain, repudiation, and vilification of a program that has made some measurable strides toward equality but which barely even brushes against the status quo? They do it by exploiting ignorance of the facts and catering to the fears steeped in that ignorance. By portraying race preferences as ripping apart rather than stitching together the economic and social gaps that define race relations today. By fomenting resentment over what paltry gains have been made.

"Given the history of this country, it is a virtual certainty that without affirmative action, racial and sexual discrimination would return with a vengeance," said Harvard professor Cornell West in his provocative book *Race Matters* (Beacon, 1993). "Even if affirmative action fails significantly to reduce black poverty or contributes to the persistence of racist perceptions in the workplace, without affirmative action, black access to America's prosperity would be even more difficult to obtain and racism in the workplace would persist anyway."

All said, opposition to affirmative action—when it offers such modest advantages to fellow citizens who only want to participate in the American Dream—is a wickedness supreme. Refusal to share the fruits of that dream is the height of inhospitality.

Meanwhile, about that stigma: It appears to be quite useful to the antiaffirmative argument, but its promoters should know that it is not very effective in discouraging the wards of affirmative action. If it comes down to a choice between the ridiculous assumption of inferiority and the chance to have a job, go to school, or get a contract, believe me, the stigma is moot.

Only the hard core among the antiaffirmative action crowd will claim that racial discrimination has been extinguished. O'Shea, for example, theorizes that discrimination is most likely a figment of black imagination, stirred up by deep-seated anger and hypersensitivity. As a result, in O'Shea's mind the black malcontent flounders in the workplace. "Even if he is somehow able to keep his resentments to himself and nevertheless radiate cheer, his internal state is likely to impair his performance, even if his talents and qualifications are of the highest order."

I include such foolishness not because it is worth pondering, but to demonstrate how the affirmative action debate has been distorted. The going philosophy among the policy's opponents is that, in the event of discrimination, a wronged party can turn to investigative government agencies or to the courts. Which means the damage has already been done and may have been done in a way that can never be repaired or recompensed. Once lost, some opportunities are lost forever.

After writing critically about a racial row in Alabama in which a high school principal discouraged a couple from attending the prom because they were an interracial pair, I received a letter from "D.K.K." of Vienna, Virginia. He described himself as a business executive, well educated and well heeled. When, he wanted to know, might black people accept that we are inherently inferior, lowlifes with weak morals and no respect for "normal" values, as evidenced by our "failures" in education and economic advancement. Why would we not be content to populate the servant class and surrender our futile aspirations for higher economic ground? he wondered. It was the cast-down-your-buckets routine anew.

If and when vacancies occur within his company, do you suppose it is likely that D.K.K. will hire a black man or woman, given his seething bigotry? Fat chance. D.K.K.'s attitude may be repulsive, but it must be examined and diagnosed before it can be corrected or punished. Such attitudes tend to leak into the environment, poisoning opportunity and hope, but the source and extent of the nefariousness often exist below the radar. Too often, it escapes—unchecked and unpunished, too slippery for the law's feeble, clumsy grasp.

Chapter 9

Sticker Shock

As the twentieth century dissolved into the twenty-first, a curious new term latched onto America's racial politics. It was new shorthand for a complex and timeless injustice: a black person's inordinate risk of being stopped by police and harassed, questioned, detained, arrested, or worse on the suspicion of criminal intent. Police called it "profiling." But black Americans, neither impressed nor fooled by law enforcement's innocuous-sounding language, came to call the experience "driving while black."

The deluge of illegal drugs and law enforcement's desperation to stem the flow gave impetus to the practice of profiling. Unscientific, subjective, and specious, profiling employed a composite of stereotypes to create a sketch of the "typical" drug dealer and trafficker. Police and prosecutors concluded that young urban blacks, particularly males, were the most likely culprits.

Though flawed at its core, profiling allowed law enforcement to step all over personal liberties. In some cases, it was an officer's license to commit verbal harassment, intimidation, and physical abuse.

Controversy over the practice came to a head in New Jersey. For many years, black- and brown-skinned motorists in the Garden State had complained of being unfairly subjected to traffic stops and detention on what seemed to be nothing more than a lark. The charges resounded throughout black neighborhoods where everyone seemed to have a first- or secondhand acquaintance with profiling's sting. But the general population ignored the cries until an April day in 1998, when four young men from New York—three black and one Latino—drove their rented van onto the New Jersey Turnpike.

To this day, the passengers say they can think of no legitimate reason the two white state troopers ordered them off the road. They do not know why Officers John Hogan and James McKenna opened fire on them, wounding three, two critically. They do not know why Hogan and McKenna handcuffed them and shoved them into a ditch while awaiting the paramedics. They cannot fathom a good reason. They could only think of a bad one: driving while black.

For a time, New Jersey state police officials denied that profiling had any role in the pullover or the violence that ensued. Police said the troopers' radar had caught the van speeding. They claimed they fired into the van because the driver had tried to run the officers down. According to the passengers, both charges were lies.

Eventually, the police story unraveled. Not only had radar not nabbed a speeding vehicle, it turned out that Hogan and McKenna's cruiser didn't even have radar equipment. Further, it was learned that Hogan and McKenna had a habit of masking the identities of their traffic stops, frequently listing black motorists as white on their police reports.

A grand jury indicted the troopers in the shootings and for falsifying official records. Meanwhile, the four victims sued. In February 2001, the state of New Jersey settled with the four young men for a total of $12.95 million.

The Turnpike story not only captured the public's imagination—and, for the four victims, a hefty sum from public coffers—it also forced the state to finally take seriously the possibility that racial profiling was indeed habitual within state police ranks and that the incidence of traffic stops involving black motorists was excessive. The state's attorney general launched an investigation, culminating in an official report, released in 1999. It found that black motorists represented 13 percent of drivers but 35 to 45 percent of traffic stops. Moreover, said the report, ethnic minorities were subjected to "heightened scrutiny and more probing investigative tactics that lead to more arrests that are then used to justify those same tactics." A damning find. Enough so that profiling was expressly outlawed in New Jersey. Then-governor Christie Todd Whitman fired Carl A. Williams, the superintendent of the New Jersey State Police, after he told the *Star-Ledger* that profiling is a "time-honored tool" and that "It would be naïve to think race is not an issue in drug trafficking." Williams later accused Whitman of "reverse discrimination"—of removing him in order to install a black superintendent. And all this, he said, "for telling the truth." Good grief.

Even after all of those embarrassments and upsets, allegations of racial profiling continue in New Jersey. Two years after the state admitted and repudiated the practice, a police officer pulled over an unarmed, twenty-nine-year-old black man who was taking his girlfriend's daughters to school. Within minutes, Bilal Dashawn Colbert had a fatal police bullet in his neck. A few days later, hundreds of protestors rallied on the state house steps in Trenton to protest Colbert's killing and to demand an end, once and for all, to racial profiling. They also pressed for an investigation of State Supreme Court justice Peter G. Verniero, who allegedly had a long-running awareness that the state police practiced racial profiling yet who, as attorney general, had made no move to stop it. Verniero was the same attorney general who wrote the investigative report that acknowledged racial profiling.

While New Jersey struggled with loss of face and public confidence in light of the driving-while-black scandals, one of the earliest plaintiffs in a racial profiling suit said the true mother of all profiling states is Maryland. For sure, the evidence backs up his claim.

In Maryland, the goldmine for profilers is Interstate 95, which can deliver a northbound traveler bolting out of Baltimore to Philadelphia in about two hours; to New York City in four.

Claiming the corridor was infested by drug-runners, the Maryland state police gave I-95 their special attention. Prodded by profiles, they stopped black and Latino drivers willy-nilly. Apparently, any black or Latino fit the bill.

Once troopers pulled over an elderly black husband and wife en route to an anniversary celebration. The couple's belongings were ransacked. The woman was denied restroom privileges. Drug-sniffing dogs were set to work. The cops found nothing.

Another day, they stopped a college student from Liberia. The officers detained the man and his passengers for hours and searched, then dismantled, the car, hunting for contraband. When they were done, the officers handed the motorist a screwdriver, suggesting he use it to put his car back together. Then they left, having found nothing incriminating.

All the while, the head of the Maryland state police insisted that profiling "was not, is not, nor will it ever be condoned" within his department. But that is small comfort to the hapless driver or passenger who knows that profilers do not necessarily require an official imprimatur to do their dirty work. And, officially sanctioned or not, the foul practice continues. In year 2000—seven years after Washington, D.C., lawyer Robert Wilkins filed a successful lawsuit against state police for an unjustified stop; three years after a federal judge discerned a "pattern and practice of discrimination"; two years after racial profiling sparked nationwide outrage in the wake of New Jersey's disgrace; and around the same time the United States Congress was designing legislation requiring states to ban racial profiling or lose federal highway funds— the state of Maryland was still racking up a shameful tally of driving-while-black incidents. The American Civil Liberties Union reported that, along one stretch of Maryland highway, blacks accounted for nearly 30 percent of drivers who were stopped, but 73 percent of drivers who were searched.

"Maryland has really been the capital of racial profiling in the United States," Wilkins told the *Washington Post*. "The disparities on I-95 in Maryland match or beat anything documented, and they've been going on for years and years and years. And they continued even after the settlement of a lawsuit and the involvement of a federal judge. How much worse can you get than that?"

No one knows exactly how common racial profiling is. But even without hard numbers, it is conventional wisdom that the practice is ordinary. The president of the National Association of Police Organizations, representing four thousand police unions nationwide, said he didn't believe it occurs. But the president of the United States was not so dismissive. In June 1999, Bill Clinton ordered federal officers to keep a record of traffic stops in order to measure the extent of the problem. When Republican George W. Bush became president in 2001, his attorney general—a proud and rock-ribbed conservative—vowed to put the screws to racial profiling. Several states followed suit, including Maryland. But not the wildly diverse, supposedly progressive California. Two months after the ACLU of Northern California opened a toll-free hotline for reporting profile stops, the group had logged 1,400 complaints. Still, Democratic governor Gray Davis vetoed tracking legislation. The state couldn't afford it, he said.

What will it take to win this small crumb of justice? Will it take another tragedy to dislodge profiling from its concrete perch? Another tragedy like the one that befell Jonny Gammage in a Pennsylvania suburb in 1996?

This is what the police said happened: They pulled Gammage over for reckless driving. He had raced his cousin's Jaguar through three red lights before being brought to heel. As Gammage stepped out of the car, he reached for something. What? A gun?

The police knocked Gammage to the ground and, while one officer held him down with a boot to the neck, the others beat him with a flashlight, a baton, and a blackjack. Jonny Gammage did not live to tell the story. He died, shackled, with his face in the pavement. The item in Gammage's hand—the "gun" that set off the police officers' murderous frenzy—turned out to be a cellular telephone.

Driving while black is no imaginary hazard. And class is not a factor. The junk heap and the luxury sedan are both red flags to profiling cops. The hip-hop kid and the sharply tailored business-man are equal suspects. Of the thirty-nine black members of the U.S. Congress, eighteen say they have been stopped and ques-tioned for no apparent reason, including Oklahoma representative J.C. Watts, the darling of congressional Republicans. Since it is unthinkable that a white member of Congress would endure such an indignity and not squeal about it, it is safe to assume none has ever had this eye-opening experience.

Racial profiling has had some regrettable fall-out effects. For example, when the National Highway Traffic Safety Administra-tion launched a campaign promoting the use of car safety belts among black motorists, the National Urban League originally signed on as a partner in the effort. But the League backed out of the deal once it learned that black drivers, especially men, were fearful that stricter enforcement of seat-belt laws would only give police another excuse to stop and search them. Although studies showed that blacks and Latinos were twice as likely to die in traf-fic accidents because they tended to not wear seat belts, the Urban League withheld its support for the safety campaign until it got as-surances from federal authorities that protections against arbitrary stops and searches would be built into safety belt regulations.

Were the danger and risk of racial profiling confined to the time we spend behind a wheel, it would be bad enough. But, it goes beyond that. As actor Danny Glover and countless black men can attest, taxi drivers pass them by as if they are invisible.

Celebrity lawyer Johnnie Cochran once put it this way: "It's walking while black, jogging while black . . . indeed, it's living while black."

That is only a mild exaggeration. Profiling pesters black Americans in every nook and cranny of public life.

There is dining while black, whereby black patrons are customarily subjected to slow service and ill will. There's even taking out while black, as in the case of a Washington, D.C., lawyer who was told to wait in the street for his pizza because deliverymen would not bring pies to the door in his all-black neighborhood.

There is banking while black, with its skittish lenders who either deny black borrowers four times more often than whites or gouge them with outlandish interest rates and other unusual terms.

There is ailing while black, which accounts for the dereliction of duty by medical professionals who fail to give black patients the full range of tests, information, and treatment commonly available to white patients. Or emergency room personnel who refuse to treat a dying black boy a few yards outside the hospital door. Some doctors and nurses employ profiling even over the conspicuously sick and wounded, I'm told. Dr. Vanessa Northington Gamble, a professor at the University of Wisconsin, tells of one hospital emergency room where it is routine to ask black male patients if they are armed. She tells of another that denies narcotics to black patients suffering from a sickle cell crisis. She says one of her own colleagues claims it is "a well-known fact" that blacks are more difficult patients than are whites. That's profiling, plain and simple.

There is enjoying yourself while black, as evidenced by the accounts of thousands of black college students who alight each spring upon the Florida shores. The police presence during the annual Black College Reunion, as the gathering is called, is noticeably larger and edgier than during the annual descent of racing enthusiasts and motorcyclists who tend, overwhelmingly, to be white. Too, the black students are corralled into certain areas of town, subjected to unusual traffic restrictions, and faced with curious hotel policies and prices that border on the confiscatory.

There is doing business while black, in which entrepreneurs, competent and well heeled enough to have been awarded broadcast licenses, cannot get a fair shake from advertisers because, as the Federal Communications Commission found, "in certain instances, the buying process is guided by ethnic/racial stereotyping, underestimations of disposable income, the desire to control product image, unfounded fears of pilferage, etc."

Sometimes racial profiling goes beyond the outrageous and is on to the absurd. Such was the case in May 2000, when Sean Gonsalves, a black reporter for the *Cape Cod Times* stopped along a highway in Eastham, Massachusetts, to interview a white evangelist who had been treading the eastern seaboard, dragging a large wooden cross and preaching to whomever would lend an ear. Throughout the interview, Gonsalves held a small tape recorder to the preacher's mouth, a common practice among journalists.

Suddenly, two police officers showed up—in response, they said, to an emergency call from a passerby who had reported a black man holding a gun to a white man's head along Route 6. Even though Gonsalves identified himself and offered his press credentials, the cops frisked him twice. When asked for an apology, Eastham police chief Donald Watson refused. He and his men would not apologize "for doing our job," he said.

According to a federal lawsuit filed against the U.S. Customs Department, there is also a risk in traveling while black, particularly for black women. The suit, citing a report by the General Accounting Office, alleged black females reentering the country are twice as likely to be strip searched for contraband as are white men and women; nearly three times as likely as black men. Yet the incidence of discovery does not justify the difference.

Shopping while black may be one of the more common forms of discrimination today. In 1995, it snared a black teenager in Maryland on a visit to an Eddie Bauer outlet store. He went there to show a friend where he had bought the shirt he was wearing. When a security guard pressed the boy for a receipt—for the shirt on his back, mind you—and the youngster was unable to produce one, the store demanded that the boy remove his shirt. Stripped of his property and his dignity, the young fellow went home and told his mother. Who promptly called a lawyer. Who promptly filed suit. Which eventually resulted in a one million dollar judgment against Eddie Bauer, Inc. The jury did not find that the security guard had acted with racist intent when he seized the youth's shirt. But who doubts that a white boy under identical circumstances would have been spared at least the affront, if not the suspicion entirely?

Not long ago, black customers in seven predominantly black Maryland communities complained that a national toy store chain refused to accept personal checks at stores in their vicinity, but did accept checks at stores in predominantly white areas. The stores admitted practicing a double standard, but denied that it was racially based. The black community stores have higher returned check rates, they said. Perhaps. But the policy amounts to profiling, no matter how you cut it. By whatever name, the practice withholds the customers' foremost possession: their right to be judged as individuals by what they say or do, rather than as part of a group.

The shopping-while-black dilemma has produced untold angst for black Americans. It is why I hate when any of my children, particularly my son, go shopping without me. It is not a simple matter of having transportation, time, and money for the trip. There is something else the boy needs. He has to have his armor on. He has to have his defenses intact. He has to have his shield ready. In case the Look is fired at him. In case some silly guard or sales clerk gets it in her head that my son—my long, lean black child, my good-as-gold baby, my honest, loyal, self-respecting, smart young man—is a thief in the making, staking out his target, looking for an opportunity to snatch and run.

And so I pester him, a symptom of the heartbreak I feel for him, as captured in this column I wrote in 1998:

You might call it Blackmotheritis—a nervous disorder afflicting millions of black women with adolescent or teenaged children, particularly the mothers of boys.

It is a chronic condition of graduated severity, whose acute stage coincides with the son's puberty. When his legs grow long, his voice deepens and especially when he gets a little fuzz over his lip, the mother's suffering peaks. She knows that, from now until he has a midlife paunch and graying temples—and maybe even then—her son will be watched through the corners of eyes, over shoulders, through one-way mirrors, through surveillance cameras.

This dread has been creeping up on us black mothers all along, bit by bit, but it is full-blown now. Overcome by fear and fury that our child could be falsely suspected and accused and roughed up or taken into custody (or worse), we therefore submit to the condition's mandates. We fret and fuss and are oh, so terribly nagging.

Keep your hands out of your pockets.

Don't reach under your shirt. If there's an itch, just live with it.

Always have the clerk bag your purchase with the receipt inside the bag.

In winter, keep your jacket open.

"Yeah, Ma," the boy says soothingly. "I know. I'll remember."

It is reassuring. But I know he does not always remember.

The other day, on a brief shopping foray, while we were looking over the compact disc players, Joseph popped his hand beneath his shirt to rub a mosquito bite.

"Joseph!" I shouted. My son's name fell hard from my mouth as if it were a pain to say it.

"Get your hand . . ."

"Okay, Ma," he said impatiently, then muttered something that seemed, at once, mad and sad.

"I just don't want . . ." I began, ruefully.

"I know, Ma. I know. I'm sorry."

Poor child. He thinks he's sorry. Doesn't know what sorry is. Won't know until he has his own child whom he raised to be honest and responsible. Whom he has watched grow into just what the doctor ordered. Who he knows to be thoughtful and loving and smart. Who a teacher once called "one of the finest kids I've ever *taught." Who another sized up as "leadership material" because "he knows who he is; he doesn't give into peer pressure. You hardly ever see a kid like that anymore."*

When he sees that child have to live on tiptoes because of some stinking stereotype that hasn't, doesn't and never will fit him . . .

When he knows that ache, he will know what sorry is.

It is an infuriating condition, this Blackmotheritis. There are times when you try to fight it. Go ahead, child; scratch that itch. Zip your coat. Put your hands wherever you want. To hell with answering someone's prejudicial paranoia. You're free. Be it.

But before you say that, you envision a finger pointed at your boy. There's a scream, perhaps. Then the clopping of heavy shoes as the cops rush in, their nightsticks drawn and perhaps their guns and their flashlights blinding your boy's sweet brown eyes. And, suddenly, there's the hard, cold floor in his face and his arms wrenched behind his back and shackled.

And all you can think about is how they'd better have plenty of room in the jail that day because you, civilized woman, are going to act such a damn fool if they ever do that to your boy.

And so you tell him, "Remember. Keep your hands out of your pockets."

And he says, "Yeah, Ma. I know."

He knows, all right. He's known for a while now. Knows what it feels like to be asked to show that he has money when he barely steps into a convenience store. Knows the sound of automatic locks engaging in cars stopped at a corner where he stands. Knows about being trailed by cops when he and three or four friends are roaming the mall. Knows about being wrongly accused.

Here is a scene from his ten-year-old mind, stored for good measure and wise caution.

Eight young friends were standing on a corner in one of the wealthiest and purportedly most socially progressive cities in America. It was early evening in late summer. In the breezy cool at the city bus stop, the little group laughed and joked with one another. They were on their way home after an afternoon of movies, mounds of junk food, and hanging out.

None of the seven- to twelve-year-olds gave it much thought as the two patrol cars approached. With a police substation only a few blocks away, there was always a steady flow of patrol cars in the area. But, when the cars pulled to the curb in front of the bus stop, several kids stopped their chatter and recoiled, eyes widening with curiosity and a certain well-worn dread.

"You four come with me," said one officer, pointing out his targets. The children traded glances, most of them fearful looks but one or two had angry faces. A second officer stood with the remaining children, his hands on his hips just above the gun holstered around his waist and the nightstick jutting through a loop in his belt.

The first cop marked off a spot on the ground where each of his four subjects was to stand. Without a word between them, they complied.

"You kids take a bag of candy from that store up there?" asked the policeman, waving toward a neighborhood drug store.

"No sir," each child responded.

"Oh, I believe you do know something about it," the officer shot back. "What you got in those pockets?"

"I got nothing in my pockets," said the oldest, defiantly.

"Oh, you got nothing in your pockets?" The cop moved closer to the boy, fingering his nightstick. He tapped the boy's pants pockets with the stick, then tapped his jacket pockets. A few coins, the only contents of the pockets, jingled in response.

"What about you?" the cop asked, turning to another boy. "What have you got?" Again, the nightstick tapped and probed, finding nothing. The officer repeated the scene with the third and fourth child.

Over in the huddle where the second officer was standing guard, the youngest child in the pack struggled vainly to stifle the tears flooding his fright-filled eyes. A girl in the group put her arm around the little shoulder, trying to console the youngster. "It's okay, Tutu," she said. "It's okay." The tiny boy took a swipe at the fat streams pouring over his cheeks, dripping from his chin.

"What are you crying for?" asked the officer, with a strained, facetious tenderness. "You don't have something to cry for, do you?" The cop spun the child around and patted him down. Tutu let out a wail.

"This little boy hasn't done anything wrong," the girl shouted. By now, her trepidation had given way to an outrage that felt familiar and old. Her heart raced and her head hurt.

Surprised by the outburst, the officer froze. Then he reached for the protesting girl.

"You don't need to touch me," she stormed. "You can't go feeling all over a female!"

The cop, stepping back from the girl, kept his eyes pinned to her face as if, for a moment, he could see himself smacking her. Then he threw his hands up as if in surrender and shook his head.

"I don't think we've got anything here," he yelled to his partner.

"You kids get on home now and stay out of trouble," said the other cop, returning to his patrol car. The vehicles pulled away slowly, then disappeared around the corner.

Watching this brief city drama was a similarly sized group of white adolescents and teenagers gathered in the parking lot of a fast-food restaurant directly across the street from the bus stop. Some of the kids were schoolmates of the black youths. Seeing that the cops were gone, they ventured over to the black kids who were trying to collect themselves and console one another.

"What were they hassling you for?" asked a white boy.

"They thought we stole some candy," came the answer.

"This candy?" the white boy said, holding up a clear plastic bag full of individually wrapped confections. Then, with a chuckle, he turned and strode down the street, his giggling friends in tow.

If such a travesty can occur in these modern times, in broad daylight, in a city that prides itself on social enlightenment, to young children whose only crime is to fit a prejudicial profile, then it can happen anywhere in America. Cochran was right. Living while black is risky business.

And make no mistake, it is blackness itself—color per se—that lures the devil to the door. Ask Amadou Diallo, if only you could. It was his black form standing in the doorway of his own apartment building the New York City cops saw that awful night in February 1999. It was his black face that peered at them, full of fright and confusion. It was his black hand that reached for the wallet in hopes of proving that he was not the young, black male they were looking for, but rather an innocent man—the earnest immigrant with the menial job he had taken to inch his way into the American Dream. It was Amadou Diallo's blackness that led the cops to see the wallet as a gun, leading them to fire upon that black form forty-one times, sinking nineteen bullets into Diallo's flesh and bone. Diallo could tell us a thing or two about living while black. If only he weren't dead, rushed to the grave by men armed with guns and power and profiles.

The news and entertainment media have had a hand in the propagation of stereotypes. In their own way, they practice racial profiling too. When children see blacks on television, 35 percent of the time the characters are doing "bad things," according to a survey of adolescents and teens of all races. The "bad things" incidence for white television characters was 9 percent. How could perceptions be otherwise, when the face applied to drug abuse and trafficking, to welfare, to crime, to teen pregnancy, to prostitution, and to academic sloth is, more often than not, a black one, notwithstanding statistical truths. When we agitated for change from the Mammies and Step 'n' Fetchits, the Mandingos and Super Flys, the Kingfishers and Calhouns of yore, it was not our intention to replace their images with more modern or sophisticated versions of buffoons, sexual predators, and criminals.

The widespread transmission of deviant or dangerous black images accounts for more than the occasional inconvenience or embarrassment. It has also produced grave injustice and close calls. One occurred in October 1989 when Boston police answered a distress call from a white motorist named Charles Stuart. They found Stuart, bloodied and seemingly in shock, in his car. His pregnant wife was slumped beside him, dead from a gunshot wound. Stuart told the officers a black man had robbed and assaulted the couple. For days, police conducted a roundup of young black men in the area, questioning and harassing them about the Stuart shootings. In the end, police determined that Stuart had killed his wife and wounded himself in an elaborate scheme to collect life insurance proceeds and free himself from familial obligations. Cornered by evidence and tip-offs, he eventually killed himself, so case closed. But considerable damage had been done to whatever peace and tranquility there had been in Boston's black community. Its residents were reminded anew of how easily people swallowed and acted on the "black-man-did-it" scenario.

Almost to the day, five years later, it happened again when a young woman named Susan Smith told authorities in Union, South Carolina, that a black man had robbed her of her car and sped off with her two young sons in the backseat. For days, the nation fell to its knees, praying for the safe return of the little boys and the swift apprehension of the alleged black thief and kidnapper. Then, police scuba divers found Susan Smith's car in a lake with the children's bloated bodies inside. As it turned out, their own mother had driven them to their deaths. For that, she was sentenced to life in prison. But, again, the "black menace" portrait had been framed and hung on the wall.

Black Americans can claim a share of the seedy underbelly of American life, but it is by no means our franchise. Until the media portray black Americans in the full range of human behavior, they are coconspirators in the profile game.

In the aftermath of the Susan Smith atrocity, and recalling the Stuart case and other instances of false accusations against black men, Tom Teepen, a nationally syndicated columnist and correspondent for Cox Newspapers, wrote insightfully, "The Black Man As Beast is a figure embedded in the pathologies of American racism. He lurks, for racism's sufferers, just below the surface even of placid lives, an indistinct but coiled force, ready to break through at any moment to terrorize and harm."

Nashville civil rights activist Tim Wise called it "the racialization of danger." In a published essay he wrote, "Consider the way we talked about the Simi Valley trial of the white officers who beat Rodney King. What is it called today in popular discourse? 'The First Rodney King Trial.' But Rodney King wasn't on trial. White cops names Briseno, Koon and Powell were, but how many Americans even remember their names—the names of the criminals involved?"

Wise said that whites are encouraged to think of crime and danger in terms of black and brown. "This process encourages discrimination against non-whites, skews our criminal justice priorities, and diverts our attention from larger threats to our well-being." As Wise discloses, statistics show we are more likely to be hurt or killed by spouses, lovers, family members, or neighbors of the same race than by "one of them."

Because profiling is so pernicious and ubiquitous, we occasionally anticipate it where it doesn't exist. We can be prickly, sometimes, having been burned so often by the nasty images and lowliness that stalk us. Like a toxic fog, it can cloud our vision, this sad expectation, and when that happens, our rage may spill over on even those undeserving of its fire.

The nation's capital is a chocolate city. Outside the federal triangle where so much of the world's business is transacted, Washington, D.C., is home, primarily, to black Americans and other people of color. Local government is mostly black, but the white-dominated U.S. Congress is the ultimate authority presiding over the city's affairs and that makes for a shaky and difficult governance. Thanks to a steady wind of resentment over Congress's refusal to recognize the District of Columbia as a free-standing entity, it does not take much to set the residents' teeth on edge. Simply put, their arrangement too closely resembles the old plantation system, when whites controlled the fate and future of black charges. Whites in city government are suspect too.

So, when a white city official griped that budget appropriations were "niggardly," he unwittingly ignited a blaze of controversy. Never mind that the word means "cheap, miserly and stingy," it was just too close to that infamous invective. Citizens complained, demanding that the official be fired. The newly elected mayor, a prim black man who is warily regarded by grass-roots organizations, went into full knee-jerk mode. When the brouhaha erupted, the mayor was still licking his wounds from protests that he was not "black enough" and did not share the passions or interests of the community at large. Apparently to prove otherwise, he demanded his aide's resignation. And then blistered by attacks of political correctness, the mayor soon rehired the official, saying he had acted hastily.

Likewise, context was ignored in a Brooklyn, New York, public school when a white teacher assigned her predominantly black and Latino third-grade class to read Carolivia Herron's book, *Nappy Hair* (Knopf, 1997). *Nappy Hair* is the story of a little black girl whose hair is coarse and curly—nappy. Far from ridiculing the girl's hair, the author, a black woman, celebrates it for its strength, resilience, and abundance.

But when word got out that Ruth Sherman had pushed *Nappy Hair* on her students, black parents revolted. White commentators were aghast. "In a story explaining the controversy, one of the networks offered pictures of shampoo advertisements featuring flowing, shiny Caucasian hair. This is the American standard of beauty, went the explanation, and blacks feel excluded from it," wrote Mona Charen, as sniffy and out-of-touch a conservative as they come. The protestations against the book, wrote Charen, were "profoundly silly, the mark of people with too much time on their hands and not enough true trouble to offer perspective."

I'll grant Charen this much: from those comments alone, she established herself as an expert in the "profoundly silly." While I agree that the parents were off the mark on this one, Charen and her ilk fail to appreciate the caustic effects of long-running images that imply, and sometimes assert, the power, privilege, and supremacy of that which is white, hair texture included. Her statement about "not enough true trouble," when applied to people of color and poor people, is arrogant, nefarious tripe. At worst, the protestors were paranoid. But it is a paranoia stoked by real clashes with stereotypes and profiles.

Once in a while, the paranoia is of comical proportions. Like the time I took my seat in the first-class cabin of an airplane with a chip on my shoulder. Since most people fly coach class, and certainly most black people do, I braced myself for quizzical looks. I noticed a flight attendant inching my way.

"May I have your boarding pass, please?" he said, kindly.

I flinched, fighting back the impulse to let this guy have it. My mind ran a preview of the argument. *What, a black woman can't be in first class? What about the white passengers' boarding passes; have you checked them? Where is my proper place, back in coach?* I bit my tongue.

Seemingly oblivious to my unease, the attendant took the boarding pass stub, placed my coat on a hanger and strung the stub from the hanger's hook. "Wanna make sure I give you back the right coat," he said, cheerfully.

It's times like this that one is grateful for the little angel that counsels restraint. Had I said aloud what I was thinking, I would have made a fool of myself. I would have made a ridiculous scene. I would have wrongly incriminated a man who, rather than succumbing to stereotypes, was trying to be helpful and efficient. Yes, black sensitivities do go haywire sometimes.

Let us understand why. Try on this analogy: One man takes a glass of water to another fellow. But as he draws near, the water bearer dashes the water in the other guy's face. Another person comes forth with a glass of water and he too throws the water on the waiting man. It happens again and again. Finally, someone approaches with a glass of water, fully intending to hand it over. But, just before he gets there, he trips and the water splashes all over the waiting man.

Don't you see? After all he's been through, it's mighty hard for him to believe that the last spill was an accident.

Chapter 10

A Room of Their Own

On a midspring morning in 1999, in a picturesque town nestled at the base of the Colorado Rockies and adjacent to Denver, the state's most famous city, two teenaged boys went berserk. They went to school that day with killing on their minds.

Dylan Klebold and Eric Harris had previously sneaked explosives into Columbine High. They had planted crude but powerful bombs and incendiary devices in lockers and cubbies, beneath bleachers and desks, in restrooms, behind bookshelves. The plan was for the explosives to detonate around the school and finish what the boys intended to start, which was to mow down teachers and students with the semiautomatic weapons hidden beneath their long, black trenchcoats. The bombs did not go off, but Klebold and Harris did damage aplenty on their own. When it was over, a dozen teenagers and one teacher were dead, scores were injured and wounded, and Klebold and Harris had taken their own lives.

As details of the carnage unfolded throughout the day, the nation watched in rigid horror, aghast at the enormity of events, incredulous that such wild violence had disturbed a school, of all things, and in quiet, predominantly white, middle-class Littleton, Colorado, of all places.

Upon word of the tragedy, black America held its breath, then whispered a question: Were the perpetrators black or white? It may have seemed impertinent to the rest of America, but we needed to know the answer for our children's sake. Experience had taught us that if the young killers were black, there could be hell down the road for black children—the hell of being swept up in broad presumptions about their characters, proclivities, and basic natures. Notwithstanding our deep grief, our fears about the condition of the culture, the rising threat of violence on school grounds and what it meant for all children's security and peace of mind, black Americans found a sliver of relief in the news that the killers were not black.

A telling thing happened in the wake of the Columbine massacre. The entire country turned inward, tearing itself apart for answers, for reasons, for anything to explain how two young white boys from supposedly solid, comfortable homes and a community that prided itself on old-fashioned values and religious fealty—two boys with whole lifetimes ahead of them—became so possessed of anger, so diabolical, so obsessed with revenge, so obedient to evil, so racked with hatred. We investigated the whole of modern American culture. Was it television programming, rife with gratuitous violence and sex? Could it have been the seedy, violent video games the boys favored? Is that how they learned to kill so cavalierly? Might alienation from, and bullying by, the school's in-crowd have had anything to do with it? What about music, like the raging, screeching rock they preferred? Had a satanic cult consumed their innocence? Parental supervision, was it too lax? Did illegal drugs drive them to it? Was a chemical imbalance to blame? How about the availability of firearms, could that have been it? Did the absence of prayer in public schools leave a hole big enough for the devil to come in?

A nationwide search for answers, an all-points bulletin, was launched. Law enforcement authorities, sociologists, physicians, psychologists, educators, parent groups, students, even the U.S. Congress and the White House kicked into high gear, searching for the demons that had invaded the young minds, commandeered them, and directed the slaughter. There was consensus that some external force had compelled the boys to murder and, with all urgency and determination, the country set out to apprehend that mysterious provocateur. It was a state of emergency.

But it was a tardy declaration. Since more than a decade before the Columbine tragedy, black youths have been killing one another at dizzying rates. Beginning in the mid-1980s, the homicide rate of young blacks blasted off the charts. Funeral directors, who used to handle young bodies only occasionally by way of disease or accident, began keeping undersized caskets in their inventory and honing their skills at repairing holes in the chest and face and making young skin look as natural as possible. Support groups for mothers of slain youngsters sprang up around the country. Ministers got more calls for counsel in the middle of the night. Kids in impoverished neighborhoods that were susceptible to violence began writing down instructions for their own funerals—the clothing they wanted to be buried in, the color of the coffin, the music they wanted played at the funeral service. In one makeshift community center in south central Los Angeles, I saw an entire wall covered with photographs of slain children—some were just babies. In my hometown of Little Rock, Arkansas, a Baptist minister and community activist started planting white wooden crosses for every young black homicide victim in the city. It wasn't long before there was a field of white crosses.

Yet no state of emergency had been called. There had been no haste to discover what on earth was bedeviling black youths. No search party had been dispatched to nab the monster, to cut off the cancer that had metastasized, spelling our demise. It was as if the country had decided violence was an inherent impulse among black youths, an internal force to reckon with, while in the Columbine case it was believed to be the work of outside influences upon whose capture the country was intent.

The disparate treatments of the white and black emergencies and the failure of a white stereotype to materialize in the wake of Columbine did not escape notice. In a letter to the editor of the *New York Times,* a reader from New Hampshire wrote:

> *If Dylan Klebold and Eric Harris had been black, who knows what black kids in high schools would have been made to endure. But because they are white, it is a societal problem and something has to be done about it, including, perhaps, posting the Ten Commandments in schools! When black kids misbehave, all blacks become criminals. Thank God, it is only the color of suspicion that is black and not the color of the crime.*

That sad commentary spoke for many.

Lest we seem overly sensitive about this, take a look at the cold numbers.

Across the spectrum of juvenile crime, the white population is underrepresented in arrests. Black youths compose 8 percent of the juvenile population, but account for 27 percent of all juvenile arrests for violent crime. Nearly 29 percent of all juveniles tried as adults are black. White juveniles constitute about 9 percent of these man-made adults. In a study of the California juvenile justice system, the Justice Policy Institute of San Francisco found that young black offenders are eighteen times more likely to be jailed than are whites. Black youths are twice as likely to be tried as adults. In Texas and in Connecticut in 1996, every juvenile in jail was nonwhite.

The Youth Law Center, which tracks and champions justice for our young, finds that the judicial system is indeed a two-faced beast, aggressive with black youths, merciful with whites. It yanks one out of every three young black males from the fold and holds him in prison, on probation, or on parole. Meanwhile, white juvenile offenders are more likely to be sent to treatment facilities when they go astray. One author of the 2000 Justice Policy Institute study summarized California's mindset this way: "Throw kids of color behind bars, but rehabilitate white kids who commit comparable crimes."

It must be noted here that Klebold and Harris, the Columbine High School killers, had been slapped on the wrist for previous infractions of law, where black kids might have been locked up or at least put under the watchful guard of probation officers. No such thing for Klebold and Harris, who concocted their murderous scheme and put together their bombs and secreted their weapons and marched around the school in unusual, curious garb with impunity. Yet black kids are treated suspiciously when they braid their hair or wear baggy pants. One of my kid's friends, a young fellow named Dante, once barely escaped suspension from school when a teacher caught him drawing something on the cover of his own notebook. Gang scribbles, the teacher surmised, threatening to send Dante to the dean's office. The sketchings were, in fact, the abstract doodlings of a rather talented, fledgling artist, signifying nothing more than the treasure of his own imagination.

White Americans are fixated on gangs and it is somewhat understandable. Certainly gang violence has made American life edgier, chancier. Although drive-by shootings were introduced by the legendary gangsters of the 1920s and 1930s—white killers like Al Capone—the hit-and-run style of murder returned to the American stage in the 1980s, largely at the hands of young black hoodlums.

In the main, white America appears unable or unwilling to differentiate between the black kids who are criminals and all the others, so a slew of one-size-fits-all tyrannies were enacted under a doctrine of deterrence and containment. Some of the laws and regulations produced under that policy were flat-out unconstitutional and outlandish. For example, for a time in Chicago, youths were prohibited from gathering on the street. This was a particular swipe at black and Latino youths who often had no other place to while away their time together. Seems the mere sight of black or brown groups of young people scared the daylights out of people, who saw the gatherings as preludes to crime and violence. After all, what other portrait of black and brown youth had they seen?

In the words of criminologist Michael Tonry, author of *Malign Neglect* (Oxford University Press, 1995), the demonization of poor urban blacks is the first step in containing, punishing, and removing them from the mainstream. The relocation plan is already well underway. The Bureau of Justice Statistics finds that, at the current incarceration rates, one in twenty American children will serve time in a state or federal prison, the overwhelming majority of them black and Latino.

At shopping malls across the country, security guards stand lookout for gang trouble, hassling or breaking up groups of youths who have done nothing more than be black, be friends, and be together. I once got mixed in with a contingent of black teenagers at a crowded mall. I suppose the guard did not spot me with my graying temples when he barked at the group, "Go home. This is not a gang meeting place." He got to know me afterward, however, when I read him the riot act and took down his name to report to the brass. Later, I gave the security supervisor what-for. Gangs are a plague, no question. But most black kids are not gangbangers and don't want to be.

The supervisor sheepishly told me he would "look into it."

When it comes to the risk of incarceration, young black Americans can expect a good deal of it. Not because they are more naturally inclined to crime, of course, but because the judicial system is more inclined to suspect them, overcharge them, and overpunish them.

A coalition of youth advocacy groups concluded in April 2000 that black and Latino youths are far more likely to be arrested, formally charged, convicted, and incarcerated in adult facilities than are white youths accused of the same crime and with identical criminal records or same lack thereof. The coalition's report—titled "And Justice for Some"—found a young black first offender six times more likely to be jailed than a white first offender. "If the system were anything like color blind," wrote the researchers, "those rates [of incarceration] would be about the same. It's clear that race is a major factor." The report found stunning differences in the way white and nonwhite juveniles are treated by the justice system, ranging from whether prosecutors decide to charge them, what they are charged with, whether probation is allowed in lieu of incarceration and whether rehabilitation services are offered—what the report called a "cumulative disadvantage" for youth of color.

The naked unfairness of such disparate treatment is one thing to decry; the fact that it is lifelong is another. The FBI says whites commit 57 percent of the nation's violent crime. Yet, blacks represent 55 percent of the country's two million inmates. (Two million! A ten-fold increase since 1972!) Here's one to rattle your tree: The incarceration rate for American blacks is four times that of black men during apartheid in South Africa, where racial justice was nonexistent.

These are not figures the American public likes to hear. Or, if it hears them, it does not seem to care.

A popular trend that affects black males has been to make more room for daddy (and son and husband and brother) in prison. Prison-building has become a new industry. Many of the facilities are being built in predominantly black or rural communities where, ironically, the locals are seduced by the promise of jobs. Boscobel, Wisconsin, for example, rakes in about nine to ten million dollars a year from its sparkling new prison, known affectionately as "Super Max." That's big money, especially in a small town.

Apparently, this is the new urban and economic renewal plan: more and bigger prisons. Nearly thirty billion dollars goes to prison expenditures each year. The states are spending more on prisons than on higher education. It was just the opposite case only a decade ago.

The racial double standard is blinding on death row. Thirty-eight states now practice capital punishment, having resurrected their death squads when the Supreme Court gave them the go-ahead in 1976. Between 1977 and 1998, 500 men and women were put to death by the state. Eighty-one percent of them had been convicted of murdering a white person. In fact, the NAACP Legal Defense Fund found that 142 blacks were executed for killing whites. The number of whites executed for killing blacks? Eleven.

Of the approximately 453 men and women currently on death row as of this writing, 161 are white, 188 are black, 91 are Latino. Some states, like Texas, are zipping through executions so fast that their death rows may have been emptied and restocked by the time you read this. If past is prologue, most of the new tenants will be black or brown.

In a bold stroke, Illinois governor George Ryan imposed a moratorium on executions in his state after learning that thirteen people on death row had been exonerated as a result of new investigations or new evidence. The discovery was particularly alarming since Illinois had executed nearly that many inmates since 1976. Ryan ordered a state panel to investigate Illinois's capital punishment system to determine whether it was fairly administered. A few members of the U.S. Senate and several clergymen are trying to abolish the federal death penalty and have asked states to follow suit. But to date, the body count on death row marches on and up-ward.

Judging from the statistics, the swollen rate of incarceration and capital punishment for blacks may have less to do with a higher incidence of criminality than with the prejudices that black people are more criminally inclined, that black criminals' deeds are more reprehensible, that blacks are less amenable to rehabilitation and redemption, and that their absence from the civilian society has, at worst, no ill effects and may, in fact, be salutary. The appraisal of black life is lower. The expectation of black wrongdoing is greater. The black menace is worse than the white menace. And severe or prolonged punishment for black inmates is therefore appropriate. The emergency is no emergency at all, only life as usual. That's the message.

Much of the surge in black incarceration rates is tied to the so-called drug war. Nowhere is the disparate treatment of black versus white offenders more appalling than in the annals of drug-related sentences. Between 1983 and 1993, drug convictions grew the prison and jail populations by 510 percent. An American Civil Liberties Union study determined that, while blacks represent 13 percent of monthly drug users, they make up 37 percent of drug arrests. The reason has a name: cocaine.

Cocaine is organic, derived from the foliage of the coca plant, which the Incas of Peru grew in abundance in the fifteenth century, adhering to an ancient tradition of chewing the leaves for their analgesic and illusory effects. Eventually, European settlers traded in coca and, at one time, paid taxes on its production. By the mid-nineteenth century, American pharmaceutical companies were producing cocaine from coca leaves to put to medical use. It became a popular anesthetic in eye surgery.

Toward the end of the nineteenth century, cocaine was added to the formula for the soft drink Coca-Cola; the additive was abandoned after about five years. By the beginning of the twentieth century, some Americans were snorting the powder for fun. Suspicions about the drug grew as medical dilemmas increased. Five thousand cocaine-related deaths were reported in 1912. Two years later, the U.S. government outlawed the stuff.

But as history has taught us, we should never confuse prohibition with eradication. Law or no law, the coca plant hardly disappeared. Nor did cocaine's reputation for lifting, or otherwise adjusting, the spirits. Nor did the need for a cash crop among South American peasants. Nor did the pain and desperation of so many lonely, dejected, destitute people and their susceptibility to anything that promises escape, however temporary and exacting. The government may have banned the substance, but it failed to address those conditions that made it marketable in the first place. Government went after supply while ignoring what drove demand.

By the 1980s, America's drug problem had careened out of control. The drug proved to be more insidious than imagined. It wiped out jobs and income, health and life itself. In many a user, it boiled away goodness, industry, responsibility, and common decency. Even then, it would not let go. There was nothing some of the addicted would not do to get more of the drug. Such was the nature of cocaine—the seduction, then the disaster.

At the same time, another temptation lurked and found its mark. The money that flowed from cocaine sales was astounding. Outside the scope of government controls, cocaine trafficking flourished, unchecked by taxation or safety regulations. It was no fly-by-night enterprise either. The industry ladder included lookouts and runners, processors and baggers, dealers and importers, all getting paid and paid well. Poor folks without two nickels to rub together one year were suddenly smothered in cold cash the next, so bountiful was the loot from cocaine. The money bore its own addictions—to the good life with its fancy cars and fine houses, tailored clothing and sumptuous cuisine, plush travel and recreation, new companions and, at the upper rungs of the trade, acolytes to run your errands and do your bidding. There was power in that powder. There was opportunity and ease. There was reprieve from despair. There was a way up and out onto the fast track of the American Dream. In the absence of any foreseeable alternative, many people latched on to cocaine as their only ticket to the soiree so many other Americans enjoyed. And damn the taboos.

Like any prosperous business, the cocaine trade underwent tinkering and evolution. Like legitimate enterprises, cocaine moguls had their own research and development departments; their own product enhancement efforts aimed at boosting profits. In the 1980s these underground industrialists found a winner when they mixed cocaine powder with ammonia, water, and ether, siphoned off the ether and heated the mixture until it crystallized into the small white rocks known as crack.

The potent crystals packed a powerful punch. Now the user could get a quicker and cheaper high. In poorer communities— most often, black and brown communities—crack took over as the drug of choice. The rate of addiction skyrocketed. So did profits.

In due course, law enforcement officials—who had tried, with modest results, to lasso the unruly drug trade—homed in on crack. Frantic legislators and prosecutors collaborated to stiffen penalties and, before long, they codified a double standard. They made sentences for possession of crack cocaine set at one hundred times more severe than penalties for powder cocaine. Even though the medical and scientific communities found no appreciable differences between the two forms of the drug, the law did. Probation was the likely sentence for a person with five hundred grams of powder cocaine. But someone with five grams of crack was subject to mandatory sentencing, which most often involved incarceration. The difference had overpowering racial implications. According to the American Civil Liberties Union, "Almost 90 percent of the people in prison for crack under federal drug laws are black." The ACLU also found that white crack offenders are more often tried in state courts, which are not bound by mandatory sentencing laws that rob judges of their discretion.

Michael Cooper, a black man, is doing time in Virginia. In 1995, he was sentenced to twelve and one-half years for distribution of cocaine. He was twenty-four years old then, with a few years of college under his belt and dreams of becoming either a doctor or a chef. Cooper prefers to think of his sentence in terms of months, not years. One hundred and fifty-one months altogether. Asked how many black friends or relatives are incarcerated or have been, Michael told me the number is "incalculable . . . nearly my entire peer group."

Cooper is convinced race was a factor in his arrest and prosecution. He believes police were more intense about drug arrests in the black community and that they were more lenient in white areas. Cooper is one of a large group of skeptics who believe the deluge of illegal drugs in the black community was not happenstance.

"The powers that sponsor the continuation of the game have two purposes," Michael said. "First, to keep the black population high and incapacitated so our unity will be prevented. Second, to control the growth increase in our population as we are thus subject to high instances of diseases and murder." He is not the only one with such dire suspicions. There is a popular theory that black communities were expressly targeted as drug dumps by underworld operators while U.S. government agents either looked the other way or, in some cases, facilitated the transactions. Such collusion has never been proved beyond all doubt, but in the late 1990s, a white journalist in California produced evidence that seemed to support the theory, including documents that implicated the Central Intelligence Agency. When members of the Congressional Black Caucus got involved, federal officials had no choice but to address the allegations. They denied any role in the proliferation of illegal drugs by the Central Intelligence Agency or the Drug Enforcement Administration. Some officials suggested that anyone who believed such a thing was paranoid, outlandish, and a race-baiter.

Notably, the reporter who uncovered the alleged scheme was fired and roundly scorned by other white journalists. Yet, the possibility haunts us, swooping down on the wings of common sense and personal testimonies. We may never know for sure, but we will always wonder.

It is not exaggeration to say that the odds are stacked against black criminal defendants from start to finish. Not only are they saddled with suspicion before the crime, but they are thereafter presumed guilty of it and, in most cases, extended only discount justice. The same poverty that ushered crime into their lives will deny them the full course of justice once they are charged, tried, and convicted.

As the O.J. Simpson double-murder trial showed us, money is the mother's milk of the American criminal justice system. It buys the diligent work of competent lawyers and top-drawer experts. It buys nose-to-the-grindstone investigators. It buys special tests and evidence-gathering. It buys time. It buys reasonable doubt. It accredits that famous *New Yorker* cartoon in which a lawyer says to his client, "You have a pretty good case, Mr. Pitkin. How much justice can you afford?"

Many a suspect, defendant, and former inmate owes his or her freedom to the harnessing of DNA, the blueprint of our individuality. But scientists have not yet mastered analytical and interpretive techniques to the point where DNA testing can be done quickly and inexpensively. Therefore, it is rarely employed and it still costs more than the typical defendant can afford. The inaccessibility of such a powerful potential absolver is another strike against black defendants.

It is common practice for convicts to proclaim their innocence insistently and consistently. Many are playing mind games or grasping at straws, but some are truly innocent. Either way, many cases beg further examination. It is feasible that most cases should be revisited, given what we know about railroading, falsifying and planting evidence, and coercing suspects to confess or implicate other people.

Take Danny Brown, for example. He was sentenced to life in an Ohio prison for aggravated murder while committing aggravated burglary. For ten months prior to his conviction in 1982, he was retained in the county jail where, he told me in a letter, "authorities attempted to persuade me to plea bargain my life and name away, a sort of blackmail: plea or suffer the wrath of the court and the state." Maintaining his innocence, Brown refused to take the offer of a one- to ten-year sentence in exchange for a guilty plea.

At trial, prosecutors alleged that the victim, a woman, had not only been strangled during a violent struggle, but raped as well. A television set, stereo, and several Christmas gifts were allegedly missing from her home.

No stolen property was ever recovered. Brown reportedly bore no scratches, bruises, or other signs of a struggle. And he was not charged with rape. Why not?

"Since I am innocent, I can only assume the state tested that sperm [allegedly extracted from the victim] and upon seeing that it did not link me to this crime, concealed the test results of this sperm with the tacit approval of my counsel," Brown said in his letter. "Seeing that I am not the rapist which made it doubtful that I would be the killer, the state did not charge me with rape because it would have weakened their case before the jury. Nevertheless, the state repeatedly told the jury I raped the victim."

Brown claims to have given police his full cooperation, "believing my innocence enough to manifest the fairness I had learned about." Now, after two decades in prison, he wonders why he ever had such faith. "I was railroaded by authorities who had no concerns for my innocence nor my humanity," Brown wrote. "I did not have a chance nor did I understand all the wrong being perpetrated against me even though I could feel it and taste it. They made up evidence, lied, twisted facts and, I strongly feel, concealed evidence that would have vindicated me."

Could DNA or even simple blood analysis make a difference? In Danny Brown's case, it did. Thanks to the tirelessness and stubborn faith of Jim McCloskey, a white former businessman from Princeton, New Jersey, where he now runs Centurion Ministries, Danny Brown was freed in April 2001 after two decades behind bars for a crime he did not commit. The DNA tests that McCloskey pressed for told the tale. But suspects are guaranteed only a defense, not necessarily a good one, and they are certainly not promised a thorough one—nor a guardian angel like Jim McCloskey. It ought to drive us crazy, this possibility that innocent people are locked up or even executed before we have overturned every last stone to assure that the verdict is just. That something so plentiful as money can be so scarce for those who need it for freedom's sake is an outrage that should leave us inconsolable. Alas, it is as Johnnie Cochran once explained to *Emerge* magazine. "The color of justice is green," he said. "The absence of green is going to get you put away."

One thing is certain: a lot are being put away. Not only black juveniles and black men but black women too. Between 1986 and 1991, the number of black women sent to state prisons for drug offenses exploded by 828 percent. Overall, according to a Justice Department report, "black men and women were at least six times more likely than whites to have been in prison at year end 1997."

Despite the astonishing disparities, society at large seems to have few qualms about how it treats law-breaking people. Many a mouth has cursed the concern for defendants' rights, as if it nullifies concern for victims' rights. That's a ludicrous, even stupid, argument but commonplace nonetheless. Judging from the silence that greets complaints of discrimination against black defendants and inmates, Americans are content to live with some travesties of justice.

Perhaps they feel safely removed from the scenes of such troubles. Perhaps they are confident that more prisons and harsher sentences will solve the problem. Perhaps "out of sight, out of mind" is their shibboleth. For sure, they must not comprehend all that is at stake, for if they understood that the safekeeping and prosperity of themselves and their children are on the line, surely then they would agitate for real justice—fair, nondiscriminatory justice, which, of course, is the only kind deserving of the name. But where is enlightened self-interest?

The long-range effects of hyperincarceration are crushing. They blossom slowly, almost imperceptibly, but inevitably. The casualties are widespread. They are the children left behind by a father or mother who will be locked away while the first steps are taken, the abcs are memorized, the first bra is fitted. They will be gone throughout the T-ball and training wheel years, the acne and necktie years, the dating years, across all the memorable moments and turning points. A parent's absence and the reason for it cannot help but cut into the child's sense of security, worthiness, and hope. Who knows what temptations may overtake them without a knowing, caring hand to guide them? Who can say just what they will think of mothers and fathers or the world from now on?

And what about the inmates themselves? Most will be released some day. Is it reasonable to believe the preeminence of punishment over rehabilitation, of isolation over socialization, will make them better men and women when they come out? Are we ready for nearly two million Americans who may be penitent but not prepared to rejoin our fast-paced society with its unrelenting demands? Aren't we begging more trouble?

In a 1999 report titled "The Effect of Mandatory Minimum Sentencing on Black Males and the Black Community," Edward Blakemore of the University of Dayton School of Law issued a chilling assessment:

> *Mandatory minimum sentences are having drastic effects upon the black community. The first and arguably most important effect is that it exacerbates the problem of single parent households within the black community. When these men are sentenced to prison, they, many times, leave behind a wife/girlfriend and/or children. If they have already had children, that child must spend multiple years of his/her early life without a primary father figure. In addition, that male's absence is even more prominently felt when the woman has to handle all of the financial responsibilities on her own. This poses even more problems since women are underpaid relative to men in the workforce, childcare costs must be considered, and many of these women do not have the necessary skills to obtain a job which would pay a living wage which could support her and the children. Black male incarceration has done much to ensure that black female-headed households are now synonymous with poverty.*

Additionally, Blakemore decries the dilution of black voting strength resultant from high incarceration rates. Forty-six states deny prisoners the right to vote. Thirty-five states forbid those with past felony convictions from participating. One million five hundred thousand black men are not allowed to vote because of their criminal records. That's 13 percent of the black male population in America.

Michael Cooper, the young man imprisoned in Virginia, wants to be ready for his eventual release sometime in the new century's first decade. He will still be a young man then, still in his thirties, and it is his hope to make something good of his remaining years. But Cooper is having difficulty repairing his life. He would like to have more educational programs and training on the inside. He believes television programs should be limited to educational viewing. He wants prison officials to de-emphasize games and recreation and pay more attention to intellectual improvements.

"In this prison, I am a member of the black majority," he told me. "However, having been in a facility where white and Latino were the majority, I notice a disparity in the quality of living conditions [medical, food, shelter] and government-sponsored educational programs."

And mandatory sentencing must go. "By eliminating any consideration of the factors contributing to crime and a range of responses, such sentencing policies fail to provide justice for either victims or offenders," says the Sentencing Project. "Given cutbacks in prison programming and rates of recidivism of sixty percent or more for released prisoners, the increased use of incarceration in many respects represents a national commitment to policies that are both ineffective and inhumane."

Advocates for inmates have not merely leveled charges against the system, then dropped the ball. They have come up with new ideas for stemming crime that should be welcomed news considering the failed performance of past and current practices. The recommendations would appear to be no-brainers in light of what we know about human nature, but there is fierce resistance to anything that does not crack the whip even louder and faster. Not even the facts about expense have moved the stubborn pro-prison crowd. Apparently it has not occurred to them that they are disgustingly inconsistent in their complaints about "throwing money" at public schools and their eagerness to liberally commit their tax dollars to new prison construction. The coexistence of crumbling schools and sparkling new jails is a testament to the lies we have told ourselves about our basic goodness and fair play. More money for schools is called a waste. More money for jails is called an investment.

But look at the common denominators among the incarcerated population. Two-thirds never finished high school. One third were unemployed when they were arrested and had incomes of less than five thousand dollars a year. Well over half were under the influence of alcohol or drugs at the time they committed the offense. Among women inmates, 36 percent reported being physically or sexually abused during their youth.

Obviously, if America harbors any hopes of sustaining prosperity, there is no other option but to focus on prevention rather than turn all of its attentions to punishment. Congressional hearings, special panels, White House initiatives, and expert studies may be helpful and validating, but we do not need them to ferret out the triggers of crime. Intuition alone is remarkably efficient, provided we first dispose of the notion that people are fundamentally different by virtue of race.

Once we agree that black people, like all people, need stability, opportunity, and belonging, are entitled to at least rudimentary respect, deserve the presumption of innocence, require the means with which to accomplish their goals (or at least try), and should have access to those means without interferences from bigotry and suspicion. Once we accept that circumstance, not nature, most often is the force behind criminal behavior, then the policies and customs that rob so many black people of their faith and participation in American life can be set right. And black Americans can begin making themselves at home.

Chapter 11

Livin' Large

Even in a shaky economy, there have never been times like these. The United States, the richest nation in the world, is richer than ever. There is an orgy of making money, spending money, and spending money to make money. Average Joes and Janes become instant millionaires on television game shows that give away huge sums of money because they draw viewers who draw advertisers who fill the coffers. Nineteen- and twenty-year-old athletes routinely sign multimillion-dollar contracts that allow them to buy massive houses, luxurious cars, tailor-made clothes, and part-ownerships in restaurants, haberdasheries, and sports teams. Entrepreneurship, Internet technology, expanded world trade, and an excited stock market produce billionaires who, scant years ago, were in junior high. These are a fast, furious, and seemingly unstoppable new rich. People of all stripes hold tickets to the financial soiree. They are making money and spending it with abandon, honoring, and accelerating, the American tradition of conspicuous consumption.

These are the good times. So good that the Federal Reserve has constantly tweaked interest rates, like a thermostat, to keep the economy from overheating. So good that the National Urban League, one of the nation's oldest civil rights organizations, closed the twentieth century with the proud declaration that "the economic state of Black America has never been healthier," a claim borne out by the numbers. Blacks enjoyed record low unemployment and record high home ownership. The percentage of blacks below the poverty line fell. Black buying power neared the five-hundred-billion-dollar mark. And the precursors for continued prosperity—high school graduation and college enrollment rates—climbed steadily.

But the Urban League also included this caveat in its 1999 *State of Black America:* "There is much left to be done." By many accounts, the ranks of the black middle class doubled or tripled over the past three decades. But the measuring stick may be flawed. In an analysis of U.S. Census data, statistics researcher A.J. Robinson reports that the standard income threshold for middle-class status is between $15,000 and $49,999 a year per family. But, as Robinson notes, the lower end of the scale is level with the poverty line. "It seems disingenuous to categorize those making slightly more than the poverty line as members of the black middle class," Robinson said. "Even using the misleading income range . . . the percentage of black families within this bracket in 1970 was 56.3 percent or 11,667,612 people. But in 1994, the percentage had declined to 46.7 percent or 13,309,033 people; a decline of 9.6 percent!"

Meanwhile, there was a tidy increase in the percentage of

higher income black households. Between 1970 and 1994, those in the $50,000 to $75,000 a year range increased by about 5.7 percent and now make up about 20 percent of all black households. They are the "true winners," Robinson says. "The percentage of the black population in the middle class is shrinking."

Whether the black middle class is enlarging, shrinking, or holding steady, this much is certain: discriminatory practices still stymie black progress. Black home-buyers are two to four times more likely to be rejected for conventional mortgage loans than are whites, according to both government and market surveys. When blacks do secure mortgage loans, they are more likely to refinance existing homes at high interest rates while white mortgage-holders are getting loans for new homes and at market rates. Despite crackdowns on so-called redlining, home ownership among blacks stands at 45 percent while 72 percent of whites own their own homes.

Overall, there remains a screaming economic gap between white and black households. In their award-winning 1995 book, *Black Wealth, White Wealth,* scholars Melvin Oliver and Thomas Shapiro refer to studies showing that "blacks have anywhere from $8 to $19 of wealth for every $100 that whites possess." What that means for financial security is frightening. "Just 65 percent of white middle-class households possess a large enough nest egg to maintain their present living standard for at least one month, and 55 percent could last at least three months," Oliver and Shapiro report. "In unmistakable contrast, only 27 percent of the black middle class has enough NFA [net financial assets] to keep up present living standards for one month, and less than one in five households could sustain their lifestyles for three months."

And get this: "At poverty living standards, 35 percent of the black middle class might last one month." Appalling.

This is a serious indictment of both past and present and a dark predictor of the future. Sparse net wealth means there is nothing to pass on, so ensuing generations will have no financial head start. Even this late in our history, it is the rare black American who has an inheritance of any significance, thanks in part to practices that suppressed his ancestors. For all practical purposes, inheritance is a white thing. Oliver and Shapiro say bluntly:

> *Inheritances are not likely to concern many African Americans. The historical reasons for this state of affairs are crystal clear. Segregation blocked access to education, decent jobs and livable wages among the grandparents and parents of blacks born before the late 1960s, effectively preventing them from building up much wealth. Until the late 1960s few older black Americans had accrued any savings to speak of, as they likely had working-class jobs. Without savings no wealth could be built up.*

For untold numbers, hard work, determination, faith, and inventiveness have been deployed against disadvantages, turning the tide and setting black families on the trail of the American Dream. When it happens, it usually happens this way: The slave begets the sharecropper who begets the factory worker who begets the college graduate who, at last, breaks the cycle of poverty and deprivation.

But it is not all right that millions of black Americans have no shot at the Dream and strive below its radar. It is not enough that more blacks than ever are skiing, traveling, yachting, draping themselves in silks and fur, playing the stock market, manning the helms of major corporations, and sitting in judges' and senators' and cabinet chairs. It is not all right nor is it enough, because, for the majority of black Americans, it is foolish even to dream about regattas and villas and brass-plated executive suites. The odds of having them are equal to a snowball's chance in hell. Not because they have no talent or ambition, but because they are systematically denied what it takes to get those things, although the country fails to see it that way. "More families have been pushed upward," said researcher Robinson. "But we have not filled their places with families from the lower classes."

The flip side of the rosy U.S. economy is a dire, depressing scene—crippling poverty and miseducation, aimlessness, homelessness, hopelessness, illness, violence. Need, need, need. This is the America many black Americans know. Despite the speedy ascent of the U.S. economy, one-fourth of black Americans live below the poverty line. Black unemployment stands at three times the rate for whites. Nearly 22 percent of black Americans have no health insurance. If there were ever any intentions to include them in the economic gala, their invitations must have been swept under the rug of apathy, selfishness, and finger-pointing. What makes it worse is that their chances of getting in are less than ever because the success bar is so high, owing to advanced technology. Reaching and maintaining a middle-class life requires more and more specialized and higher education—an increasingly expensive proposition—for which the poor are ill-prepared. Their children languish in public schools that are most likely to be overcrowded, crumbling, and neglected, if not despised, by those who can afford better.

Many owe their subsistence to public assistance programs,

which are minimal and restrictive. But a large number are known by a term that seems, on its face, oxymoronic: "the working poor." They are not equipped with computers, family sedans, deeds, stock portfolios, or even health care policies. They have no savings, nor hope thereof, and can barely stitch together what it takes for food and shelter. They have jobs, maybe two or three, but their wages are not enough to boost them into the mainstream. Worse, their impoverishment is, in and of itself, a lightning rod for prejudice and discrimination. It is not uncommon for poor job applicants to be passed over because they live in blighted neighborhoods which, according to popular assumption, are bastions of laziness and criminality. A case in point: In 1995, Speaker of the U.S. House of Representatives Newt Gingrich called on blacks to stop being poor—a fine idea if only it could be accomplished by fiat. "You have to learn new habits," he said to black America. "The habits of being poor don't work." Of course, Gingrich's quack cure gave no heed to the "habits" of discrimination and myth-mongering that paved the way for much of the loathsome poverty. But he didn't stop there. He betrayed his ignorance and arrogance further by asserting that "African Americans have no history of entrepreneurship and economic development." Although he taught college history and fancies himself a historian, Gingrich showed what a sorry one he is, ignoring the proud history of Reconstruction, when black Americans, freshly freed from slavery, built businesses, schools, farms, and churches, got elected to office, including the United States Congress, and established full-service, independent communities. He did not take into account the habits of the Ku Klux Klan and those of state legislatures that produced the Black Codes, nor did he recount the duplicity of national leaders like

President Andrew Johnson, who conspired against black achievement and overturned black advances through terror, threat, and prohibition. He conveniently overlooked the Harlem Renaissance, that famous era of black literature, scholarship, music, and art. He did not consider the habits of Jim Crow, white flight, redlining, and discriminatory covenants and their annihilative effects on black industry and self-determination.

His history lesson certainly excluded the Tulsa, Oklahoma, community of Greenwood, once nicknamed the "Black Wall Street." It was affluent, especially for the times, bolstered by three dozen black-owned businesses. But it only took twelve hours one night in 1921 for angry whites, led by the Ku Klux Klan, to annihilate the community. The Black Wall Street and three hundred black lives were lost in the rampage. Eight decades would pass before the state of Oklahoma entertained the idea of reparations for the destruction of Greenwood. But by then, the inheritances and head starts of Greenwood's legatees had long been obliterated. I guess Gingrich forgot about that.

Nor would it have been useful to his argument to include the late nineteenth century riots in Wilmington, North Carolina, where blacks had established a thriving, independent community along the Cape Fear River. As prosperous blacks gained political clout, whites in the area grew more and more nervous. By the 1898 election, black-white relations had become so taut that, on Election Day, many blacks were kept from the voting booths by intimidation and threats. After the election, a black activist was told to leave town or be lynched. The Wilmington Light Infantry and Naval Reserve marched through the streets of the town, looking for the threatened man. When the troops did not find him, an angry mob set upon the black town, burning homes and firing shots. Between 120 and 150 people died in the riot, most of them black. Survivors left town in droves, closing their churches, law offices, stores, restaurants, and barber shops. The property they left behind was redistributed among the white townspeople and the new city government obliterated records of prior ownership.

Gingrich also failed to reference the fate of black farmers, who constituted 14 percent of the nation's farmers in the 1920s, but less than 1 percent today. In 1997, black farmers sued the U.S. Department of Agriculture for discrimination. For years, they were denied USDA loans and other assistance earmarked for the keepers and tenders of the soil. One such farmer, a tobacco grower in southern Virginia, said the department lost his application papers, bedeviled him with delays and mistakes in processing, and restricted access to the money he was able to borrow. He was unable to get his crops in and out of the fields on schedule. The farmer was among five thousand blacks slated to each receive a fifty-thousand-dollar award in a consent decree that settled the class action suit. But, the Virginia man says there will be no farm to pass on to his children.

Not only did Gingrich overlook those examples of black independence and commerce, the boastful "historian" did not even seem to know the history of black enterprise in Georgia, the state he represented in Congress. Had he researched the matter, he might have come across Donald Grant's excellent account, *The Way It Was in the South: The Black Enterprise in Georgia* (Birch Lane, 1993). This one passage from the book might have stilled the speaker's tongue:

Many free Negroes were skilled workers and some acted as independent contractors. Favored slaves were carpenters, blacksmiths, coopers, metal workers, seamstresses, cooks, and teamsters. Some were able to parlay these skills into small businesses after the Civil War; in fact, blacks dominated the skilled-artisan work at first. Since whites no longer had to compete with the unpaid labor of slaves, they gradually moved into these occupations. The increased competition gave impetus to Jim Crow laws that began in the 1880s. One goal was to force blacks from the more desirable jobs that were beginning to elevate some of them into the middle class's lower ranks.

The historical record belies Gingrich's claim time and time again. From the start, black industry has been evident and utile. And throughout the country's history, black enterprise has been foiled by white resistance. One of my son's high school history textbooks notes, "A Virginia planter who rented his slaves to an iron manufacturer complained that they made money by working overtime and got the habit of roaming about and taking care of themselves." The planter, the text said, put a stop to that.

If, during his matriculation, Gingrich did not have access to the bounty of research and records about black enterprise, he might have dug up Quintard Taylor's work, *In Search of the Racial Frontier: African Americans in the American West, 1528–1990* (W.W. Norton, 1998). There, he might have been schooled by this passage:

Mary Ellen Pleasant, perhaps the most celebrated black property owner in antebellum California, owned three laundries and was involved in mining stock and precious metals speculation. John Ross operated Ross's Exchange, a used-goods business, while James P. Dyer, the West's only antebellum black manufacturer, began the New England Soap Factory in 1851. Former slave George Washington Dennis managed a successful livery business in the city. Mifflin W. Gibbs, who arrived in San Francisco in 1850 with ten cents and initially worked as a bootblack, in 1851 formed a partnership with fellow Philadelphian Peter Lester to operate the Pioneer Boot and Shoe Exporium, a store that eventually had "patrons extending to Oregon and lower California."

From Taylor's book alone, Gingrich could have learned about the numerous benefit and relief societies established by and for blacks in the American West; about the Antheneum Institute, which was a center of black intellectual life in California; about Abner Hunt Francis and his mercantile store in Portland, Oregon; about the four hundred black-owned businesses established in Houston, Texas, by 1915 and the creation of Houston's Negro Chamber of Commerce in 1946.

Gingrich might not be expected to recite the names, dates, and places of all black achievement on the business front; no one could. But, then, most don't claim to be historians and most don't regale a national audience with tales from the crapper. Most don't have the bully pulpit of the U.S. House speakership and most don't have the incentive he should have had to get his facts together before addressing such a serious topic.

Verily, Gingrich's oversights served his blame game well. His ridiculous diagnosis underscored the popular sentiment that the poor are poor by their own hand and that only under their own steam will they rise out of poverty. Gingrich's prescription? "If you're black you have to work harder and if you're black and poor you have to work twice as hard." He said it matter-of-factly, with a that's-just-the-way-it-is shrug.

Such believers do not take into account the institutional and attitudinal barriers to black achievement, nor their roles in the maintenance of those barriers. Most would take umbrage at the accusation of racism or bigotry, denying any connection between the "habit" argument and the "inferiority" doctrine that has long suppressed, or at least strongly discouraged, black resurrection. After all, they would say, they hold no hatred toward black people, only wish us well and, besides, "Some of my best friends are . . ." But their habit of treating the poor as a breed apart and then imbedding that belief into law, policy, and practice has undeniable racial implications, given the woeful facts of our condition. For that reason, class warfare, as it is called, is synonymous with racial warfare. Both are vicious and full of danger, mindful of Voltaire's warning, "If we believe absurdities, we shall commit atrocities."

The reversal-of-fortune philosophy—that the *poor* are different from you and me—fails to take into account the fundamental math of human nature. When we are deprived, we are, by definition, unfilled and needy. When we are needy enough, we do not busy ourselves with life's sublimities, but its basics. When that is our preoccupation, we are likely to become desperate. When we are desperate, we may grow angry. When we are angry, we are capable of otherwise unconscionable and uncharacteristic acts because the drive to survive is so compelling. It is an unalterable equation, irrespective of race. Hence, the crime and decadence that teem in many impoverished areas are byproducts of circumstance, not of race. Indeed, where they exist, drug use, drug dealing, robbery, and sexual promiscuity offer a certain sad logic. The need for escape, for income, for the exercise of acumen, for comradeship, for the release of anger, for pleasure, for some form of power are immutably human characteristics. What is illogical, what defies human nature, are the unsung millions of poor people—the majority—who do not succumb to these temptations, but rather lead lives that would qualify as exemplary in even the best of circumstances. It is our great disgrace that prejudice, stereotypes, and ignorance are so staunchly arrayed against them. Should America ever decide to rid itself of the scourges of crime and decadence, it will purge poverty, that great corrupter of the human spirit. But first, it must face its own complicity. It must face its own bad habits.

President Lyndon Johnson's War on Poverty, launched in 1964, and subsequent antipoverty campaigns helped alleviate some of the worst suffering. Hunger and disease are far less common now than fifty years ago, but they are by no means vanquished. In the Mississippi Delta, in Appalachia, and on Indian reservations, for example, poverty still stalks the terrain like a predator, turning the lives of young and old into an unending fight to survive until tomorrow, when the struggle begins anew. No savior, no miracle is on the horizon. They were born, have lived, and will in all likelihood die without so much as good hope to pass on to their children. And this, while the country can barely keep count of its riches.

The country trained its sights on urban poverty in the 1990s, designing and executing a legislative ruse called "welfare reform." Reducing the public assistance rolls, and thereby the cost to taxpayers, was championed by Bill Clinton in his 1992 race for the White House. The Democrat pledged to "change welfare as we know it." At the time, the familiar face of welfare in America was a black one, despite the fact that, numerically, whites on public assistance considerably outnumbered blacks. However, the percentage of blacks who are poor has always been disproportionately high. So when they wanted to humanize the issue, news reporters and camera crews rushed most often to black doorways, focused on black faces in the welfare line. And the myth prevailed.

In 1994, when Republicans gained control of both the U.S. House and the Senate for the first time in decades, they enthusiastically assumed the welfare reform mantle and tinkered with a plethora of plans including one, promoted by the aforementioned speaker Newt Gingrich, to place the children of welfare mothers in national orphanages where they would, ostensibly, be eligible for private adoption. Never mind that black children are low on the adoption totem poll. The proposal again bespoke an attitude of "otherness" about the poor, as if the poor child is dispensable, is loved less, than the child of means. Again, Gingrich turned away from the history of human nature that had, only recently, affirmed the potency and constancy of parental love in faraway Rwanda, where tribal warfare had chased millions of refugees into filthy, disease-ravaged corrals. There, in the most squalid and disgusting conditions imaginable, emaciated women cuddled their hungry babies, offering withered breasts in a futile attempt to give the children the leanest chance of survival. When medics tried to take their children for treatment, the mothers fought fiercely until they were assured they would have their children back. These were women who had almost nothing to begin with and had lost that small bit to death and destruction, with little to no prospect of recovery. But their children were still their treasures.

Did Gingrich and his cohorts really believe that an American mother, a child of the Land of Opportunity, would easily part with her child merely for lack of provisions?

What eventually came from the lengthy, fluctuating welfare reform debate was a 1996 law that ordered able-bodied recipients to work. States, now authorized to manage their welfare registers, imposed strict time limits for benefits, limited cash allowances, and tightened food stamp qualifications. Accordingly, the labor- and job-training markets burgeoned while welfare enrollments declined. On the surface, welfare reformists had a hit. Politicians marveled at the dwindling rolls, crowed about the savings to taxpayers and patted themselves on the back for their engineering feat. They paid no attention to the other story of welfare reform—the one that left poor young children without day care or with too little to eat now that their mothers had been shoved into the workplace. The braggarts of welfare reform did not take into account the costs of working—transportation, child care, and clothing. They did not consider the newly employed who had to string together part-time jobs to make ends meet—positions that offered no group health insurance or other fringe benefits. While the number of prison cells tripled in the last thirty years of the twentieth century, public housing was available for only one in four eligible poor families. The dirty little secret of welfare reform was hidden behind a whitewash of good news.

As the so-called reforms take root, social scholars see a catastrophe in the making. In an on-line forum in November 1996, Dr. William Julius Wilson, a Harvard University sociologist and author of *When Work Disappears: The World of the New Urban Poor* (Knopf, 1996), predicted "we will be facing a major problem in our inner cities" since the new welfare reform law prescribed jobs but did not provide them. "Welfare recipients will be flooding a pool already filled with jobless workers," Wilson said. "This could result in the creation of a huge number of homeless families—the worst kind of dependency."

For black Americans, the welfare reform trends are foreboding. The new law has been most beneficial to white recipients, who in many instances have been able to find more decent jobs and find them quicker than people of color. That should surprise no one; "last hired" is an American routine. Now, for the first time, not only the percentage but also the raw number of blacks on welfare has exceeded the figures for whites in some states. Civil rights advocates are not being prickly when they worry about the future of a predominately black welfare state and how it will feed old stereotypes.

By no means should these reservations imply that the welfare system, as we knew it, was viable. It was a cruel entrapment that fueled dependency, discouraged the family model, and encouraged people to settle for less. For black people especially it was a corrupt bargain: Take these handouts and stay on your side of the road.

But the cold turkey approach to "ending welfare as we know it" is rife with wrongdoing of its own. Rather than offer incentives that build confidence, buoy optimism, and give recipients the gratification of achievement, welfare reform pulls the rug out from under the poor. It's an ultimatum, a weapon. The stick rather than the carrot.

That some people deserved the shove goes without saying. There are cheats on the welfare rolls just as there are on country club rosters. But sink or swim is a helluva message to give one's fellow Americans. What is most frightening is the leeway allowed the individual states. They already have orders to downsize their rolls by increasing percentages each year or else lose federal funds. But, under the law, a financially strapped state or one overrun by arch-conservatism could conceivably cut welfare benefits to its nub. Or end them completely. The awfulness of that possibility should be obvious. Its feasibility should be too. Poor people's political power is slight to nonexistent. They have no campaign contributions to withhold. They have no political action committee endorsements to ransom. They are not sought out for political punditry or con-sultation. They are mere pawns in a foul game of political expedi-ency and populist pandering. A charismatic demon in the state legislature or the governor's office, under the guise of reform, might well persuade his constituents to tear welfare asunder.

Fortunately, an army of social activists remains vigilant and on guard against further erosions, but their power is limited. They, too, are at the mercy of political winds. In short, the poor are trapped in a society that reserves its regard and its privileges for producers. For owners. For haves. Everyone else is considered a drain on the culture, a burden to bear, an interloper. In these having-it-all, getting-it-all times, even the sense of noblesse oblige is becoming extinct. They call it "compassion fatigue" these days— a gentle term for not giving a damn.

If America still considers it a self-evident truth that all men are created equal, that they are endowed by their Creator with certain unalienable Rights, that among these are Life, Liberty and the pur-suit of Happiness, as Jefferson declared in 1776, then poor black Americans have more than a minor point of contention. To the de-gree that the U.S. Constitution seeks to ensure those rights, poor blacks can argue that they have been deprived of their Constitutional guarantees. The chokehold on liberty is evident in the national habit of quarantining people of color by housing patterns and mortgage discrimination, by the epidemic of failed public schools, by transportation shortages, by job discrimination. These restrictions automatically restrain the pursuit of happiness.

And what about life itself? Black Americans have, as always, the lowest life expectancy, the highest infant mortality rate, and the highest rate of death from treatable illnesses of any ethnic group in the country. For black youths, the picture is stunningly critical. The 2000 U.S. Census finds that 30 percent of black children are in the high-risk category as determined by poverty, their parents' employment and educational level, health care, and their home environments. Comparatively, 6 percent of white children are defined as high-risk. More than one million American youths are trapped in neighborhoods of extreme poverty, with more than 40 percent of the households below the poverty line. Nearly 75 percent of those kids are black or minority races. The black male child is particularly endangered. Black males between ages fifteen and twenty-four are five times more likely to die from firearm injuries than are white males the same age. And AIDS, a heartless killer, has turned on the black community with brute force. The Congressional Black Caucus has called the epidemic "a state of emergency." As if those developments are not disturbing enough, the Centers for Disease Control and Prevention reports that the suicide rate for black teenagers now stands at about 8.1 per 100,000. Twenty years ago, the rate was half that.

There is no genetic predisposition to these conditions. They are the work of circumstance. And in many ways, those circumstances are the work of discrimination and racism. In a bold initiative, U.S. Surgeon General David Satcher has called on the medical community to study the effects of stress and racism on health. Dr. Satcher and the National Medical Association say mistrust of white society, the pressure on black citizens to assimilate, battling discrimination and coping with prejudices and slights are taking their toll on the physical, mental, and emotional health of blacks.

The theory may strike some as preposterous, especially those who have not discerned the drone of racism that vibrates through the black world. They may not be attuned to it—it may be below their radar—but if they will stop and listen, they may be surprised to find how constant a tone it is. The National Medical Association, the largest organization of black physicians in the country, says that American medicine is bedeviled by racism. "We must dispense with the misguided belief that medicine is value-neutral when, in fact, the medical community reflects and even reinforces prejudices and values of the larger society," says the University of Wisconsin's Dr. Vanessa Northington Gamble. Gamble notes unsettling disparities in the treatment of black and white patients. In some areas of the country, she said, whites are seven times more likely to have heart bypass surgery than are blacks for whom heart disease is a tireless killer. Gamble also reported that pregnant black women are less likely than whites to receive information about the adverse effects of drinking and smoking on their unborn children; and blacks are routinely excluded from clinical trials used to determine appropriate treatments for an assortment of illnesses.

When it comes to the environment, racism's role in endangering black health is inarguable. To easily locate the toxic waste dumps, incinerators, petrochemical plants, brown fields, landfills, and lead smelters that service American industry, head for the poorest and blackest part of town. Take the predominantly black Fourth Ward of Houston, Texas, for example. Black people compose 28 percent of the city's population. But reverse that figure and you will have 82, the percentage of the city's waste matter that ends up in the Fourth Ward.

Then there is Convent, Louisiana, a black community in St. James Parish, nestled against the Mississippi River between Baton Rouge and New Orleans. The people there used to live off the land by farming, hunting, and fishing. Then a succession of petrochemical plants, grain elevators, fertilizer plants, and oil refineries— drawn to the river for its transportation advantages—moved into the Convent area (140 of them in all) and now the people of Convent are plagued by persistent sinus troubles, headaches, upset stomachs, respiratory ailments, and other serious illnesses, including cancer. It is scarcely a coincidence that the rates of disease and illness are so high there now. Indeed the cases are so plentiful that lovely little Convent is now a part of what the locals call "Cancer Alley."

Winona, Texas, is the home of two commercial hazardous waste injection wells. Conditions there became so intolerable after the wells began operating that the townspeople were driven to organize M.O.S.E.S.—Mothers Organized to Stop Environmental Sins. Phyllis Glazer of M.O.S.E.S. once described the area to a congressional hearing.

"Odoriferous emissions came from the facility, accompanied by burning eyes, nose and throat, nausea, vomiting, seizures, spontaneous nose bleeds and shortness of breath," she said, noting that a significant increase in rare cancers, birth defects, spontaneous abortions, brain and liver damage coincided with the facilities' arrival.

Despite cases like those and the suspicious onset of medical maladies coinciding with the introduction of industrial pollutants, federal, state, and local governments are still skittish about the correlation. For the most part, industry insists the health problems are either coincidental or highly exaggerated. Scientific studies about environmental factors and the occurrence of "sick clusters" are often inconclusive, much to our annoyance and perhaps our endangerment. Notably, however, chemical plants never even consider locating in well-to-do areas, where it is foregone that the citizens would use their considerable clout to kill any such plan. Upper-class home-owners may not be ready to concede the link between chemicals and illness, but they are plenty clear that they don't want the plants in their neighborhoods.

This is where poverty and racism collaborate to make a true misery. Industrialists settle in poor neighborhoods because land acquisition is less expensive, the residents can offer little resistance, owing to their impoverishment, and the political forces, drooling over the prospect of growing the tax base, pose no objections. When they make the pitch to the neighborhood—if they do—it is in the name of economic promise. The plants will bring jobs to the area, they say, fully appreciating what a temptation that is where joblessness abounds.

Nationwide, three to four million children live within one mile of a site that has been designated by the Environmental Protection Agency as hazardous. Most of those children are black and Latino. In the face of such naked disregard, how can these millions possibly feel at home?

Chapter 12

Fools Rush In

The past decade brought a spree of black-bashing literature so well received that one has to wonder whether racial harmony is not only overestimated, wishful thinking, but a ruse—a distraction, as the smiling face is to the knife-wielding hand.

A cadre of conservative American scholars has been busily restoring old models of white superiority at the expense (by definition) of everyone else, but most especially of black America. For the most part, their demeaning "research" is merely a revival of ancient quackery about brain size and genetic variations that, according to these self-styled experts, prove black people are physiologically inclined to academic mediocrity, crime, idleness, and hyperactive sexuality. Generally, they have concluded that the average black intellect is sub par, that a mere 16 percent of black Americans have IQs exceeding one hundred, and that the African lineage is cursed with genetic coding that renders our brains, and thus our brain power, inept while oversizing our genitals and sexual appetites.

Several of these "race scientists," as they're being called, have connected alleged racial inferiority to crime, teen pregnancy, and violence rates, charging that the black family and black culture are so demented that it is our "arrested development," not racism, standing between us and the American Dream. Dinesh D'Souza, an author and conservative think-tank operative, portrays slavery and segregation as beneficial to blacks—rescue missions, as it were, from our supposedly degraded natural state. Further, D'Souza suggests that black people have little or nothing of significant value to bring to America's table. Indeed, D'Souza argues that the legendary "melting pot" ideal is itself foolhardy. "Multiculturalism," he said flatly, "is based on a denial of Western cultural superiority."

D'Souza's message is that black Americans have essentially three choices: to take stronger doses of Anglo-Saxon influence and approximate whiteness to the utmost; to accept that we are substandard and prospectively subservient guests on American soil; or to brace ourselves for exclusion and privation, the wages of noncompliance.

Obviously on a mission, these propagandists can be quite insistent, pressing their credentials upon audiences as if a curriculum vitae were infallible and the Ivy League never produces the occasional idiot. Too, they often become indignant when their work is questioned or ridiculed, though the challenges hardly shake their argument. They are married to it, for better or worse. Witness this letter from one such race scientist who beseeched me, a black woman, to accept his preposterous IQ propaganda. The mailing included a batch of articles about black inferiority.

For a long time now, the reaction to work of this kind has been to give it the silent treatment if possible and hoot with derision if silence is not possible. This will not make a serious body of scientific work go away.

Racial differences are a subject that the United States will eventually have to grapple with. This information—and the differences in achievement that it explains—are not going to go away just because the subject is an unpleasant one or because we refuse to face it.

I suspect that you are committed to an egalitarian view of race and that your views are not likely to change, no matter how convincing the evidence to the contrary. However, I hope that these articles will help open your mind to the possibility that we race realists are serious people with serious reasons for holding our views.

The writer of the letter is a graduate of Yale, one of the nation's most prestigious universities. He is not a racist of the fire-breathing kind. If he has supremacist tattoos, they're not visible when he wears a business suit, his usual public attire. This man is not known for harsh or foul language, threats or violence. Rather, Jared Taylor comes off like a gentleman—a little stiff and loopy, perhaps, but otherwise seemingly civilized. Taylor once spent an hour on a Washington, D.C., television talk show trying to get me and another black commentator to swallow his sour pulp—his "scholarship"—about black intellectual inferiority. Taylor repeatedly tried to flatter us, allowing that there are exceptions to the inferiority paradigm and that we were glowing examples of that departure from the norm.

It reminded me of a famous story from the 1940s about a black woman invited to a white woman's house for tea. After exchanging pleasantries and small talk for a while, the hostess was overcome by a newfound and unexpected ease she felt with her guest. She burst forth with what she intended as a compliment. "You just don't seem like a Negro," the white woman said. "Thank you," gushed the black lady.

That was then. Taylor's two-faced "compliment" went nowhere. Had there been any evidence of black stupidity, I told him, it was that the show's black producers and hosts had invited someone like him to the show and given him a forum for his drivel. Undeterred, Taylor sent me his "race realists" letter a few days later.

The Frenchman Julien Benda was not just a pithy essayist; he may have been a prophet. His assessment of public passions in pre–World War II Europe causes one to wonder, in hindsight, if the man didn't have a crystal ball. Benda's seminal work was a warning bell about the travesty of intellectual prostitution in the midst of public discord. He called it *La Trahison des Clercs* (The Treason of the Intellectuals).

According to Benda's thesis, the assorted ideological factions in Europe—the various Us and Thems—were, at first, annoyances to free-flowing discourse on the continent. Later, the groups—self-segregated by ideology, religion, and nationality—made noise and mess, injected tension, and set up torrid competitions for power and privilege. Benda put the flashpoint for war at the moment the intelligentsia became disloyal to objective truth, shucked their disinterest, and began taking sides. Then, the factions became "a compact impassioned mass." Flaunting their biases, the scholars, thinkers, and orators of the time gave the factions a new lease. Grassroots activists were emboldened by the high-brow rhetoric, writing, and purported research. The intellectuals legitimized the people's prejudices, escalated them, and hardened their resolve to act. Thus, the "treason" against the traditions and obligations of intellectualism to uphold truth dispassionately. A decade after Benda wrote *La Trahison,* Europe was at war.

Were he here now, the essayist might have similar misgivings and warnings about the new nest of traitors abroad, this time in America. Dinesh D'Souza and Jared Taylor have company galore.

They are an industrious bunch, these turncoats. They rage against immigration, rising birth rate, and settlement by non-whites. They bemoan the demise of the white majority. They fear that manifest destiny is in jeopardy—that is, the ultimate manifest destiny of white supremacy. Academic racists know that many white Americans are anxious about losing control of the population and of the institutions of government and capitalism. But rather than lend their expertise and talent to educating the dread-filled white populace, thereby mitigating the problem, they are fostering hostilities with an outpouring of provocative "scholarship." Adding insult to injury, they invariably submit their work as "objective." Most are not nakedly racist, but their cover is pretty transparent.

University of Maryland professor Edwin A. Locke, writing for an Ayn Rand Institute publication, even attacks fellow intellectuals for not joining him in his derision of multiculturalism. "In this age of diversity-worship, it is considered virtually axiomatic that all cultures are equal," wrote Locke. "Western culture, claim the intellectuals, is in no way superior to that of African tribalists or Eskimo seal hunters. There are no objective standards, they say, that can be used to evaluate the moral stature of different groups."

Locke "absolutely" disagrees with what he calls "cultural relativism." Locke names "three fundamental aspects in which western culture is objectively the best. These are the core values or core achievements of Western civilization, and what made America great." Locke's three touchstones are reason, individual rights, and science and technology.

"In contrast, it was precisely in those Eastern and African countries which did not embrace reason, rights, and technology where people suffered (and still suffer) most from both natural and man-made disasters . . . and where life-expectancy was (and is) lowest. It is said that primitives live 'in harmony with nature,' but in reality they are simply victims of the vicissitudes of nature—if some dictator does not kill them first."

For good measure, Locke assures his readers that the ascendancy of Western culture—which is to say, the white man's way—"is not an ethnocentric prejudice; it is an objective fact." He makes only a fleeting reference to the culture's transgressions and failings and, when he does, Locke dismisses them as aberrations. Nazism, he says, was "too incongruent with Western values to last" and, besides, the West "corrected it." Locke names slavery as another Western mistake. But, he points out, Westerners didn't start it.

Of course, there is no discussion of Western colonization and pillage across the globe. Nor any mention of how such devilry oppressed native cultures. Nor a word about the wicked reasoning, abuse of individual rights, and annihilative science and technology deployed against those "others."

Like many of his ilk, Locke is shaken by challenges to white culture, or "Western civilization," as he puts it. "Its core principles are under attack from every direction—by religious fanatics, by dictators and, most disgracefully, by Western intellectuals, who are denouncing reason in the name of skepticism, rights in the name of special entitlements, and progress in the name of environmentalism." This can only lead to chaos, according to Locke.

The executive director of the Ayn Rand Institute echoes Locke. "Some cultures are better than others," wrote Michael Berliner in one of the Institute's publications. "We should honor Western civilization not for the ethnocentric reason that some of us happen to have European ancestors but because it is the objectively superior culture."

Both Locke and Berliner claim ethnicity is irrelevant to culture. But that ignores the fact that a culture is a creation of its people and that people are the guardians and purveyors of the culture. When Berliner wrote about the "sham of preserving one's heritage," he must have seen Western culture as an accident. From his writing, culture is not something to preserve, but something to discover. The values Locke and Berliner espouse are commendable and fruitful, but Europe did not hold the patent to those values and they are not the exclusive property and practice of European Americans.

Glayde Whitney, a Florida State professor known for his theories of congenital inferiority, has not been deterred by the outrage and denunciations that have greeted his work. His mill is in full swing, producing heaps of fodder for the racist soul. Claiming that blacks account for no more than two percent of the "intellectually qualified," Whitney says equality is an unreasonable, even hazardous, objective.

"Blind adherence to an egalitarian fallacy has driven a dangerous stake of divisiveness into the heart of America," writes Whitney. "The failure of honesty in facing uncomfortable truths is getting worse rather than better." One of those truths, according to Whitney, is that black people are inherently and immutably inferior and should be tolerated only to the extent that we concede to white demands.

In their infamous 1994 book, *The Bell Curve,* conservative think-tanker Charles Murray and academic Richard J. Hernstein not only advanced the low-IQ line on black people, they managed to insult one of black America's proudest institutions in the process. The authors noted that historic Howard University in Washington, D. C., is responsible for nearly two-thirds of all black college graduates. But, adds Murray, "this school is not considered to be difficult." From this, we are to believe that even the institutions designed to remedy our allegedly innate intellectual poverty are, themselves, inept. For sure, these fellows know no shame.

What is their purpose? What do the Lockes, Berliners, Whitneys, Murrays, D'Souzas, and Taylors expect us to do with their findings? They do not propose genocide per se, or any other means of weeding out what they see as human chaff. They have not recommended racial partitioning of this country or a "back-to-Africa" movement. But, the collective effect of their work certainly suggests the murder of ideas and customs and, most important, the concept of achieving equality. To hear them tell it, that is a futile and wasteful endeavor. Whitney mocks outright those members of society who may be trying to accommodate diversity. "Instead of facing uncomfortable truths and coming to grips with real issues, let us continue to acquiesce in the egalitarian fallacy," he taunts. "As sensitive and caring people we must continue to meet racist extortion with policies of appeasement. After all, a policy that worked so well on the international scene at Munich in 1938 will certainly work equally well on the domestic scene in the year 2000."

In light of all that, turn again to Benda:

The modern [intellectuals] are the moralists of realism. They are not content to remind the world that harshness is necessary in order "to succeed" and that charity is an encumbrance, nor have they limited themselves to preaching to their nation or party what Zarathustra preached to his disciples: "Be hard, be pitiless, and in this way, dominate." They proclaim the moral nobility of harshness and the ignominy of charity.

Provided we were tempted to abandon the quest for equal standing—and, of course, *never*!—what would the intellectual marauders have us do instead? Since only a few who pose as intellectuals dare to invoke the "go back to Africa" refrain, they obviously expect us to make our adjustments here. Given that, the logical enactment of their philosophy can only be our self-subjugation—that is, they want us to give up our vanity, accept our indigence, and find contentment in our lowly estate. Other than to abet and fortify the doctrine of white supremacy, what other purposes would that serve?

In studying the "clerks" of his day, Benda considered a set of ulterior forces:

The imposition of political interests on all men without any exception; the growth of consistency in matters apt to feed realist passions; the desire and the possibility for men of letters to play a political part; the need in the interests of their own fame for them to play the game of a class which is daily becoming more anxious; the increasing tendency of the "clerks" to become bourgeois and to take on the vanities of that class; the perfecting of their Romanticism; the decline of their knowledge of antiquity and of their intellectual discipline.

If academic racists benefit from their foul play, we do not. The elevation of one culture over others is a lethal exercise, never more so than in the world's most ethnically and culturally diverse nation. The prejudiced, treasonous teachings spell danger. We were warned by Benda and we should be haunted by Voltaire's admonition, "If we believe absurdities . . ."

Chapter 13

My Country 'Tis of We

On matters of race especially, America suffers bipolar afflictions. On the one hand, she hails the mix of peoples that make her unique among nations, the very thing that may account for her unequaled power. On the other hand, she seems bent on forgetting, as quickly and completely as possible, the assorted cultures that Americanism comprises. Just the term "multiculturalism" is enough to raise dander in some quarters, as if it is an affront to the republic. Some Americans are simply irritated by the infusion of ethnic iconography, adherence to ethnic traditions, and adoption of ethnic identifiers. They are especially unhappy that some of us choose to acknowledge both our past and present. To them, terms like "African American," "Asian American," and "Latino American" are something approaching heresy, decidedly *un*American.

Having been born when we were called "colored" or "Negro," I adopted "black" when it became popular at the end of the 1960s.

I preferred it to the then newly revived "Afro American" designation because "Afro" was what I called my hairdo. I have stayed "black" in spite of the latest construction, "African American," for two reasons.

First, it is my blackness itself that America needs to confront, not my continental origin. When an immigrant from Guinea named Amadou Diallo was gunned down in February 1999, it was not his Africanism that rattled the four undercover police officers, leading them to unholster their weapons and fill him full of lead nineteen times. It was Diallo's blackness that shook the cops. I want America to understand that I am not weary of my ethnicity, am not burdened by it, am not fretful about it, do not want to forget it, and will not run from it.

Secondly, while I admire the concept behind the term "African American," I am bothered by its ambiguity that, to me, defeats the purpose. As we learned some years ago, black people do not hold the franchise to African American. A white woman in Pennsylvania named Teresa Heinz proved this when she pranced through the political arena as an African American. Ms. Heinz was born and reared in Mozambique so, technically, her claim was legitimate. But it riled black Pennsylvanians who believed the candidate had used disingenuous tactics to woo black voters. Heinz apologized for her insensitivity and dropped the reference. As far as I am concerned, she could have held on to the name. And I will keep mine, confident that it cannot be co-opted.

I am certainly, permanently, and exuberantly a black American, proud of both halves of my identity—the former, representing my heritage, the latter, my ideology. I am both a child of Africa—with its communalism, spirituality, artistry, its love of nature, its veneration of family—and a daughter of America, with its reverence for the rights of sovereign individuals to exercise that sovereignty. To ignore my ethnicity is to forsake the powers that inform and propel me, the labors of my ancestors and the debt I owe them, the gifts with which I am culturally endowed, and the continuum that sustains me. To ignore my nationality is to betray freedom's champion, for it is this country, my country, that bids me to unleash my native self and, by its creed—even if not by its history—grants the license to be, to try, to win. Black and American. Black American. A fantastic synergy; the two are better than each alone.

Accordingly, I am not attracted to the "color-blind" society that has been so dreamily promoted. It is, in my view, anti-American. This nation would not be itself without its amalgam of peoples. The potpourri of ethnicity, religion, and nationality is what separates America from every other country on the globe. Indeed, it is the definition of America. To reject it—to turn a blinded eye to it—is to spurn America herself.

Still, I understand what they're getting at, these color-blind enthusiasts. They want race to be an incidental factor, an afterthought, a neutered agent with no influence over our rights to life, liberty, and the pursuit of happiness. But it is America's role to see to that. Ethnic pride is no threat to the ideal. Rather, it is its proving ground, its test pattern, its calibrator, its thermometer. Race keeps America honest and authentic and ticking. Without it, it's just another country.

Rather than color blindness, why not color love? Why, by now, have we not resolved to celebrate, cheer, relish, recognize, explore, honor, and appreciate the respective races and their treasure troves? Lord knows, it would surely work wonders in calming the country's jagged nerves. Lord knows, too, I am ready to wallow in my blackness and my Americanness. To sing "Lift Every Voice" and "The Star-Spangled Banner" with equal fervor. To wrap myself in the red, black, and green flag of black liberation and to salute Old Glory too. To recite the Pledge of Allegiance without feeling like a hypocrite or a fool when it comes to "indivisible, with liberty and justice for all." I believe I speak for the masses when I say that black Americans are ready to relax and be at home in America. And to ask, when will America welcome us?

It is said that black is not a color but a state of mind. Undoubtedly so. We have, after all, a rainbow all our own. Deep chocolate, mocha, copper, peanut-butter brown, rusty red, creamy yellow, pearly pink—these are the skins we're in. Blackness is the experience, the heart and soul, wrapped inside the complexion.

Of course this makes no sense to children, literalists that they are. Years ago, there was a boy in my neighborhood—a little white boy visiting his grandparents for the summer—who came to our house every morning, beckoning my children to play. They spent hours together, indoors and out, a roving cluster of energy.

Once the little fellow ran in for a cool drink and, as he gulped down his juice, he began to tell me about his near-future plans. He would be returning home soon, he said. He would miss my kids because he didn't have many kids his age in the neighborhood back home. Said his parents did not allow him to play with older kids. Or with black ones, he added.

"Well, what about my kids?" I asked him, taken aback.

He turned the cup up one last time, took a swallow and said, pointedly, "They're brown." Then he skipped off to play.

That was an object lesson in color blindness. But outside the range of early childhood, race has implications. It does mean something that is significant, owing to human contrivances. As Harvard's Cornell West has asserted, *race matters.*

At this juncture, I am not concerned what all accounts for the differences. The nature versus nurture debate is, for practical purposes, moot. For whatever reason and by whatever hand, black America has a set of cultural markers that is unique. Where heritage ends and environment begins and how they interact is irrelevant to the reality of our lives.

Our wants, needs, joys, and sorrows come from a common reservoir of humanity, but the manifestation of those forces is, in some ways, determined by our peculiar experiences. And that determines how we act out the magnificent drama of being human.

For generations, black Americans led separate lives from other Americans. Law and custom ordained it. First slavery, then segregation held us apart. But the isolation enforced by man did not, could not, neutralize the human nature endowed by the Creator. So, during the long partitioning of black from white America, we simply established our own methods and styles of satisfying our spirits, borrowing liberally from our ancestors, both near and far removed, and employing our own ingenuity.

Everything from how we worship, the names we give our children, what we eat, the way we style our hair, the music we make, the disciplinary tactics we employ, how we dance, and how we communicate with one another was produced by the confluence of African tradition, passed along by practice and word of mouth, American circumstance, and Eurocentric influences. Necessity was the mother of our inventions, and segregation was the mother of that necessity. Together, they produced a hybrid, part African, part American.

It is regrettable that the subculture that emerged from our shut-out society is so widely misunderstood and, worse, reviled. At bottom, we have the same objectives as anyone else: to be safe and healthy, to love and be loved, to produce for posterity our strong, happy children imbued with knowledge and with faith in themselves, to enjoy simple pleasures and, occasionally, splendid ones, to contribute and be appreciated for it, to have a hand to hold at life's twilight, to die with the peaceful assurance that, somehow, it mattered that we were here.

Thus, when white America lights a unity candle and black America jumps a broom, each upholds the custom of marriage. That fundamental sameness, that extramural truth, should cancel the ridiculous race competition. Alas, many Americans are bothered by the difference, failing to see the identical objectives underlying the dissimilar techniques.

As the walls of separation erode and blacks and whites are exposed to one another in more ways and more often, America is becoming more receptive to these incidental differences. Or at least more accommodating. But, to quote the poet, there are miles to go before I sleep.

Whiteness, both a state of mind and a power source, still disturbs the quest for color love. It imposes its vanities upon nearly every aspect of American life, insistent that whiteness is the best way or the only way and that all others constitute dissidence and degradation.

In a bold, incisive book titled *White Reign: Deploying Whiteness in America* (Palgrave, 1998), Peter McLaren, a white professor at the University of California at Los Angeles, put it this way: "Whiteness displaces blackness and brownness—specific forms of nonwhiteness—into signifiers of deviance and criminality within social, cultural, cognitive, and political contexts."

Most white individuals depart from the directive now and then. Some do so most of the time. A few wonderful souls seem thoroughly withdrawn from the race game, bless their hearts. But, seeping from the individual members are fear or anger, mistrust or resentment, dislike or hatred, and these negative feelings tend to coagulate until a large clot is formed, cutting off the free flow of alternatives, whether by design or by happenstance.

United by common experiences and beliefs and bonded by the human predisposition for protecting its collective interests, individual Americans tend to split off into power or action groups— white America, black America, Latino America, Native America, etc. As the largest of these groups, white America has always called the shots, often in total disregard of all others. In many ways, the majority has exercised its prerogatives with tyranny, forcing its cultural standards upon the entire nation and marginalizing, even demonizing, smaller power groups who were merely following their own road maps en route to an identical destination: the American Dream. Whiteness has narrowed the way, cut off alternative routes and, for sure, slowed the traffic. Now that America is growing browner and blacker by the day, white America's grasp on the culture has turned into a chokehold.

It is disgraceful but cannot be surprising, then, that some black Americans have tried to discard their blackness in hopes of gaining easier and fuller access to the fruits of privilege, power, and esteem. Once upon a time, it was not uncommon for some blacks to "pass" for white, relying on their fair skin, straight hair, and other European features to sneak them across the color line. In the 1959 movie *Imitation of Life,* a fair-complexioned, straight-haired black girl named Sarah Jane succumbs to the temptations of whiteness and launches a double life—a white girl to the outside world and a black girl who lives with her live-in-maid mother by night. The movie makes the point of how ludicrous and tragic Sarah Jane's pretense is, but it also showcases the supreme advantages of whiteness. The Caucasians in the movie are glamorous, beautiful, rich, and the ones with power. Sarah Jane's mother works for them. Even though the white family falls on hardscrabble times, it is just a matter of time before things look up and the world is again at their feet. "Imitation of the High Life," they might have called it.

During the pre–Civil Rights era, some blacks whose physical features precluded passing for white resorted to other avenues for reprieve from their blackness and the troubles it posed. Many a cosmetics and pharmaceutical company owes at least a part of their fortunes to black men and women who purchased skin-whiteners and hair-straightening products in an attempt to mimic whiteness, to approximate it, to get as near to it as possible, even at the risk of their health, even at considerable expense and inconvenience, even at the price of their dignity.

Neither passing nor bleaching are as popular as they once were, though most black people know of at least one member of the race who is pretending. The mainstream message about the desirability of whiteness is, however, as potent and prevalent as ever, and many black Americans try to answer the call, forswearing the touchstones of blackness. It is not appearance but attitude that betrays these poseurs. Their contempt for black icons, leaders, and traditions can be pathological. They can be excessively critical of black people who do not, like them, conform to white standards, and their excoriation wins high praise from whites who are leery of black people in the first place. Compliant, submissive to and respectful of majority rule, the imitators pride themselves on "independence"— their euphemism for the self-imposed alienation from the black community at large. The rest of us, they say, are mere creatures of the pack with a lamentable and outdated focus on race.

This submersion of the true self in a sea of sameness suggests self-loathing, not autonomy. It is some of the flotsam of racism and segregation that washes ashore from time to time. It is the grown-up version of the famous 1947 experiment in which black psychologist Kenneth Clark presented black and white dolls to 253 black schoolchildren, asking them to choose the good and pretty doll. Two-thirds of the children chose the white doll. When in 1985 clinical psychologist Darlene Powell Hopson repeated the exercise in Connecticut, she got the same results. Again, two-thirds of the black children preferred the white doll; three-fourths of them said the black doll was "bad."

Children can be forgiven and pitied for their sad choice. Warding off negative images and stereotypes is hardly child's play. The balance between authenticity and assimilation is a delicate one— how much of either is too much or too little? But the balance can be struck and maintained without resorting to ethnic treason. There can be little sympathy for the delusionists who only flatter and encourage white supremacy.

Whether by conquest or acquiescence, much of black culture has been replaced by Euro- and Anglocentric standards. Some of that is to be expected. But it is galling for a multiethnic democracy to insist that a group surrender its heritage and identity entirely. Yet America has made it clear that, while it is multiethnic, it does not want to be multicultural. White America's ultimatum? "Do it our way or risk ostracism, exclusion, mistrust, or exile."

True integration, the object of desegregation, would have admitted black people to the mainstream of American society without compromise. Ideally, we would have marched our black selves and black institutions and black traditions across the American landscape to acclaim. If not that, then at least without hindrance. But, there were conditions. And forfeiture of black culture in deference to white standards was foremost. In terms of recognition and respect, America is and always has been a Eurocentric monopoly.

My good friend David is quite a fellow. "Dashing" might be the word. He is handsome, energetic, charming, well educated, and an amazingly agile conversationalist. There is nothing shy or retiring about him, so when David sets his mind to something, he goes after it with unremitting, and sometimes impulsive, vigor. In most ways, David is an immensely confident man.

But more than his personality and intellect allow David to stride so assuredly toward what he wants. His whiteness gives the moves their muscle and, more often than not, it is smooth going, entailing little risk. David's privilege is imbedded in his skin. He'd be the first to admit it.

Once, on a steamy day in Washington—a city situated on swampy terrain—David got a sudden urge to go swimming. He imagined the cool, clean water lapping at his ears and how it would relax him. In short order, the thought became a plan. He made a couple of phone calls, shut down his computer, activated his voice mail, grabbed his worn leather satchel, and slipped out of the office.

David lived in a midtown apartment building that had no swimming pool, nor did he know anyone whose pool he could visit. But he did recall that a large and famous hotel near his home had a pool.

So my friend, wearing swim trunks beneath his chinos, sashayed up to the pool attendant at this large and famous Washington hotel where he was neither a guest nor the guest of a guest and announced himself as a neighbor in dire need of a swim. After a few moments of schmooze and a twenty-dollar tip, David was soaking in the blue water.

On another occasion, my wily friend abruptly changed his mind about an airline flight from San Francisco to Washington. At the last minute in the airport terminal, he decided he wanted to remain in California a few days longer. Trouble was, the flight was boarding when David made this decision. He was, however, not to be undone. Not only was David given a voucher for another flight without penalty and on the spot, but he was able to persuade airline personnel to retrieve his luggage from the plane.

As a personality type, Davids come in many colors, all ages, and both genders. There are captivating and audacious black, brown, yellow, and red men, women, boys, and girls. We native Southerners know them to be an indigenous crop. They are a rare breed that helps keep the world interesting.

But, if you tell David's stories to black folks, the standard response is some variation of this theme: that the pool attendant would have sicked hotel security on a black David whose request for a swim would have been seen as impudence, trouble-making, or perhaps mental disturbance. And that a black David in the airport scenario would have been asked to stand aside while airline officials huddled nervously at a distance, whispering with their eyes cut his way, trying to figure out how to handle their disruptive and potentially dangerous passenger who must be up to something, and was possibly even a terrorist. He would have gotten his luggage all right—upside his head, as the saying goes.

Apprised of this take on his antics, David has grown more keenly aware of the perks his race affords. He appreciates his own guile and wit, but he also recognizes how his race colors the impression he leaves behind. White man makes innocent, even delightful, mischief. Black man wreaks havoc.

David has begun to experiment with the disparity, challenging the tensile strength of white privilege and comparing it to the relatively thin and fragile strands of opportunity for others. The benefit of the doubt, the presumption of innocence, the patience, understanding, and cooperation accorded him are, David says only half-jokingly, "a white thang."

David's black counterparts would not be said to possess "dash." In the black community, the term is "flava," as in "flavor." As in spice. As in that certain savoir faire. As in a swagger and a strut, a pose, a style. As in a degree of cockiness, but not too much, and a degree of cool, but not too little. As in pride blended with self-assurance, combined with fearlessness, mixed with a clear sense of destination.

It is an authentic American dish, this mixture of European norms and ethnic flair. It is not to be confused with arrogance, although arrogance may be an element. It is not be confused with anger, although anger may be in there. It is not to be confused with militancy, although militancy may play a part.

Flava is often misread. When black males exhibit it, it disturbs white folks to no end. We saw and heard their protests in 1968 when Tommy Smith and Juan Carlos shoved their gloved fists into the air on the champions' stand at the Olympic Games in Mexico. That was black pride, not unpatriotic defiance. We saw it in the early years of Cassius Clay, the future Muhammad Ali, when he blew into the ring with so much bluster. That was more courage than bravado. Many of us have seen it in classrooms and in courtrooms and in the workplace, when some black American was called on the carpet about something and refused to hang his or her head.

Lo, in times of glory and in times of trouble, America seems to expect black people to be meek and mild, grateful for the lucky break we've gotten or for the mercy we beseech. Maintaining dignity and reserve, keeping the chin up and the head high are often taken as an offensive strike.

I saw this in action a few years back when my then teenage daughter and her boyfriend got into some trouble at their high school for violating the policy against public displays of affection. The kids immediately owned up to what they had done, acknowledged they had been wrong, asked forgiveness, and promised never to do it again. But what struck the white principal's nerve was the fact that neither of the young offenders cried and wrung their hands. "You're not crying or anything," he said in wonderment to my daughter. Later, he downright seethed at her boyfriend when the young man looked him straight in the eye. The disgust on the cold man's face was so thick it could have been scooped with a spoon.

Flava, which asserts black authority, threatens white complacency. It threatens whites' sense of being in charge and, in so doing, their sense of peace. They recoil from the assertion of black pride and power in the individual, but more so in the group.

Perhaps the country would like to break or at least break down this ethnically drenched self-assurance and to dissolve flava in black Americans. Certainly it has tried, usually by ultimatum: Do it like we do it or else.

Consequently, those who conform and mirror European models are rewarded for their achievements. Golfer Tiger Woods is a good example. The young man is already a legend, thanks to his uncanny and unmatched talents on the golf course. But, were he not Stanford-educated, a self-named "Cablinasian" (part Caucasian, part Black, part Indian, and part Asian), had he not mastered standard English, were he not a true-blue capitalist, and a calmly self-assured athlete who knows how to make his bragging sound modest instead of cocky, Tiger Woods would hardly be the darling of the sports world that he is, no matter how outstanding a player. I daresay that if Tiger Woods were more assertive and demonstrative of his blackness, with funky clothes and braided hair and street-tinged cool—if he were corn-rowed, heavily tattooed, basketball phenom Allen Iverson of the Philadelphia 76ers, for example—the media would pick him apart, looking for the hero's holes.

On the other hand, Venus and Serena Williams, the powerhouse tennis-playing sisters from Compton, California, provide some hope that the Eurocentric standard in the sports and entertainment worlds may be faltering. The Williams sisters are distinctive on the court with their tall, dark, muscular, and powerful bodies, and their braided hair, sometimes replete with beads. You can't miss their blackness. It is unequivocal, straight-up, and for real.

The sisters tore through the elite circuits of the professional tennis world, all but flaunting that blackness. Their father, Richard, had virtually bred them for the sport. After teaching the game to himself, Richard had put racquets in his daughters' hands when they were wee things on the crumbling public courts of Compton.

When at last Richard introduced his girls to the professional tour, Venus was repeatedly criticized for her alleged arrogance and "attitude." She neutered the criticisms by wearing down and defeating opponent after opponent. And only when it was evident that the Williams sisters were redoubtable champions did sportswriters amend their assessment of the women and begin seeing flava for what it was—a no-nonsense, unbowed, ain't-got-time-to-play-games approach to life. Even so, the young women still run into prejudice and bigotry from time to time in their circle, even though it is the reputedly urbane and sophisticated world of professional tennis.

The bias against nonconformity is ensconced in the popular salute to "those who work hard and play by the rules"—another of those overused phrases from the politics playbook. There is no question whose rules they mean.

Political science professor Andrew Hacker, the author of the brilliant *Two Nations: Black, White, Separate, Hostile, Unequal,* had this assessment: "Those who wish to move ahead in this world should do their best to emulate white demeanor and diction. And this in turn means that black Americans should cast themselves as the kinds of people whites would like blacks to be."

Continuing, in the summer 1994 edition of the Freedom Forum's *Media Studies Journal,* Hacker wrote:

> *Needless to say, white Americans find it unsettling that black citizens see things this way. Most whites want to feel that they have made genuine overtures, and they tell of acquaintances and workmates with whom they get on well.*
>
> *Is this simply a case of miscommunication, to be threshed out in a workshop or seminar or weekend retreat? Come now. What these black colleagues see is a reality: that for the greater part of their lives, they have been confined to a separate sphere. Save for some marginal mingling, whites live among whites, and blacks among blacks. Due to the persistence of this segregation . . . the two nations have evolved distinctive cultures. The racial division holds at every class level, so much so that even black Ivy League alumni schedule separate reunions because they feel out of place among white classmates.*

And, I would add, in that gap between the white and black communities, there grows a wild forest of misunderstanding and assumption. Including the wrong-headed view that black pride is a hazardous thing.

One of the few black institutions to survive cultural subordination is the church, the spine of the black community. Other than the family, it has always been our most prized institution, having been one of our first. And like the family, it was one of the few outlets that embraced us as we were. There, we were not lowly and unwanted, but beloved and exalted. Not even whiteness, with all its might, could orchestrate or otherwise intervene in our relationship with the Creator. So the black church was both a bulwark against mainstream tyranny and an asylum for weary, oppressed souls in sore need of nurture, fellowship, and release.

As other avenues of activism and empowerment opened, the black church lost some of its influence and appeal. When black communities disbanded and dispersed, many churches lost some of their membership. But, the black church is still basically the entity it always was—a preserve of religion, politics, and social activism. It is still a nursery for black achievers, social activists, and political leaders. Its traditions are still etched on the black psyche, so much so that even gangsta rappers who made their mark with profane, obscene, misogynistic, and violent lyrics will often begin their Grammy acceptance speeches with "Giving honor to God." The black church is still a fixture, the community center, for black America. And, as ever, it is an all but totally black institution. The reverend Dr. Martin Luther King, Jr. did not exaggerate when he called eleven o'clock on Sunday mornings "the most segregated hour in America."

Part of the reason, no doubt, is the different traditions of religious worship, particularly among Protestant faiths. To this day, the Southern Baptist Convention is overwhelmingly white and the National Baptist Convention is entirely black. They may belong to the same denomination, practice the same religious doctrine, worship the same God, and strive for the same heaven, but, down here below, they are cleaved by race.

Black spiritual expression confounds many whites. Where they consider solemnity and repose to be the appropriate religious demeanor, black tradition calls for lively rejoicing, public testimoni-als, passionate prayers, and call-and-response. So entrenched is this tradition that even those blacks who adhere to more formal reli-gious ritual—and there are many—have at least a passing acquain-tance with evangelistic protocol. Somewhere along the line, they have been exposed to hymn-raising. *I-yi-yi love the Lo-o-ord, He heard my c-ry.* They feel the rhythm of the poet-preacher and the congregational reply.

> *In the midst of a storm-tossed sea . . .*
> Yes.
> *When your ship is rocked by the trials and tribulations of life . . .*
> Um-hum.
> *Dial 911 and get Jesus on the line.*
> Well.
> *He won't be too busy to take the call.*
> Naw sir.
> *He'll tell the operator, "Put them on through."*
> My Lord.
> *Next thing you know, He'll be there.*
> Yes.
> *Stepping out on the water.*
> Come on, now.
> *Stretching out His nail-scarred hand . . .*
> Say it, preacher!
> *And whispering, "Peace . . ."*
> Peace.
> *"Peace . . ."*
> Peace.

"Peace be still."
Hallelujah!

That's the black church we all know. Even if we don't go.

We need not discuss the outrageous claims of white supremacists who argue that they are divinely chosen for preeminence
among the races. But, like them, some of the sober-minded white
people of faith are uneasy with the growing popularity of dark-
skinned religious icons. For example, the belief that Jesus Christ
was black is anathema to many white Christians who have always
worshiped a golden-haired, blue-eyed Christ. Their objections,
given the credo that Jesus was flawless in spirit and deed, bear a
strong odor of racial prejudice. The *National Catholic Reporter,* a
widely read publication, selected a black Jesus for the cover of its
millennium issue in January 2000 "to make a racially inclusive
statement," according to the artist, a woman from Vermont named
Jan McKenzie. She named her creation—a youthful figure with
dark skin and a head full of thick, corkscrewed hair, *Jesus of the People.* However, some of the people wanted no part of the colored
savior and dismissed the magazine's cover as blasphemy. One letter
to the editor at the *Reporter* blasted the portrayal as "nothing but a
politically correct blasphemous statement reflecting the artist's and
the so-called judge's spiritual depravity." It was signed "Christian
Patriot."

Carving out a home in America requires considerable energy.
Forests of racism and racial estrangement lie in the way. White
America does not know us, and its orthodoxy about black people
often qualifies neither as fact nor even sound theory. Some of it has
no more kinship to truth than the primitive belief that earth-

worms, wriggling upon the ground after a hard spring rain, had actually fallen from the sky. Rather than investigate black life and open its books to fact and enlightenment, in many instances, white Americans simply fill in the blanks with twaddle.

We are an enigma to whites. They do not see the compatibility of blackness and Americanism or how it can possibly work.

They pull back from the Million Man March without understanding that it was not a racist's call to arms that our men answered, but the yearning to regroup, to feel a part of a movement, the buoyancy of collective will and self-determination that drew the multitude to the nation's capital in 1995.

They scoff at the NAACP, the National Bar Association, the National Medical Association, and the Congressional Black Caucus without understanding that each was born of having been excluded, not as a nod to separatism but to support, advance, or reward the talented and skilled black professionals that white institutions forsook. They question our dedication to women's rights because we do not consider our men an enemy or a threat but an equal part of the struggle for equality and, in their own right, worth fighting for. They do not get our sense of humor with its irony and sarcasm and self-effacement, not understanding that these same inequities sometimes make us cry and scream. They do not know about black soul and flava and how they stir our feet and hands and hips. They cannot hear the voices whispering in our heads, urging us onward and upward—that Anyhow, Keep on Pushin', Movin' on Up voice that bids us to look back and remember but to never turn back and give in.

They turn their noses up at professional black male athletes, portraying them as performers with outsize physiques, undersize brains, and no meaningful ambition beyond showing off their extraordinary skill, creating extravagant lifestyles, accumulating sex partners, and pushing as many boundaries as possible. One author, a former network television producer named Jon Entine, even belittles black athleticism by reducing it to a mindless pursuit. Entine wrote *Taboo: Why Black Athletes Dominate Sports and Why We're Afraid to Talk About It* (Public Affairs, 2000), which argues that black athletes excel because they are better equipped biologically for rigorous sports than are whites and Asians. Intelligence, perseverance, and discipline may be factors in athletic success among blacks, says Entine, but he thinks black athletic prowess is pretty much preordained and mindless.

Jonathan Marks, a professor of biological anthropology at the University of California at Berkeley, takes serious issue with Entine's thesis. Marks wrote the following for the *New York Times* op-ed page in April 2000:

> *Controls are crucial in science. If every black schoolboy in America knows he's supposed to be good at basketball and bad at algebra and we have no way to measure schoolboys outside the boundaries of such an expectation, how can we gauge their "natural" endowments? There is a lot more to being black and being a prominent athlete than mere biology. If professional excellence or over-representation could be regarded as evidence for genetic superiority, there would be stronger implications for Jewish comedy genes and Irish policeman genes.*

Marks had this admonishment for Entine and those under his sway: "Inferring a group's excellence from the achievements of some members hangs on a crucial asymmetry: To accomplish something means that you had the ability to do it, but the failure to do it doesn't mean you didn't have the ability."

Flare-ups on the courts of play—which are surprisingly rare given the tension and high stakes of the competitions—are inevitably met with noisy outrage and grumblings about black violence. Meanwhile, hockey, a white-dominated sport, is so violence-ridden that the bloodshed has become expected and mundane. There is seldom an outcry. Indeed, the violence in hockey is regarded as benign, almost quaint, and part of the show.

If black culture is to be emancipated, the best hope rests, as usual, with our youth. They have already made inroads. In rap music, they created a whole new genre, lifting the lid off long-repressed anger and pent-up joy, hitching them to ancient rhythms and melodies plucked from the marrow. Rap is original and brazen, some of it viciously so. It can be degrading, misanthropic, violent, threatening, and vile. Some of its messages and language are inexcusable—an eruption of hostility that, in all probability, is misdirected and, by any account, self-destructive. Some of it is a vulgar display of braggadocio, mistaking audacity for courage, temerity for toughness, and self-congratulation for self-esteem. Recording artist Sisqó of the highly successful hip-hop group Dru Hill says the egotism in rap is actually a celebration of long-sought achievement. "The reason why rappers talk about all this stuff is because now they got it. And before, they [didn't]," he told a national television audience. "So they are, like, happy. They're like, 'I got the necklace; I got the ice,'" he said on the TV program *Politically Incorrect*.

For all its showiness and insolence, rap can also be tender and

206

uplifting, poignant and inspiring. Tupac Shakur, who lived dangerously and died violently, left behind several moving recordings including "Keep Your Head Up," a paean to black women.

Despite the music industry's bow to rap music at annual awards shows—not to mention record executives' eager embrace of rap's fat profits—mainstream America has extended no hospitality toward the genre nor its practitioners. Rap artists are generally seen as rebels, anarchists, and criminals, even by some black Americans.

Whatever tone of voice is given to rap, it is all genuine and true to the modern world as experienced, or at least perceived, by the preponderance of black youths. It is their poetry, their love-in, their protest march. It does not matter how many white artists enter the rap field to raise its cross-cultural appeal; rap is an essentially black outlet that challenges, even defies, the mainstream order and insists on telling its own story in its own way.

Likewise, young black Americans have turned to fashion to represent repudiation of establishment standards. Athletic wear, low-slung pants, large jewelry, braided hair, and dreadlocks are far cries from the oxford shirts, pleated trousers, and pageboy haircuts modeled by the white establishment. But these departures are purposeful. Unconventional attire has always been a tool for teenaged rebellion.

The physical appearance of black youths who adopt these hip-hop styles is, for many white Americans, a red flag that signals them to stop, look, lock, and listen. Gang lore has penetrated white consciousness where black expressionism has not. Thus, when whites see a black kid in a colorful athletic jacket or a bandanna, they often assume the wearer to be a street thug, teeming with dangerous intentions. Steve Nawojczyk, a former coroner and private investigator now devoted to helping gang members escape their hazardous lifestyles and reach for the sky, has often seen this misjudging of the book by its cover. "While many gang members wear certain types of clothing, one must be very careful in assuming that a young person is a 'banger' simply because they are wearing a Colorado Rockies or Los Angeles Raiders cap or jacket," he told me. Some kids are merely following their natural taste and preferences and have neither ties to gangs nor the desire to establish them. "Other kids who exhibit gang style are, in fact, only 'being cool' by dressing the part," says Nawojczyk.

Black boys in do-rags or corn rows and black girls with thick ropes of African-style braids fare no better. Apparently, the establishment equates the styles with militancy, and militancy with black rage. Consequently, black parents are left to quiver with dread when their hip-hoppers leave the house, knowing they are likely to be greeted with unwarranted suspicion and fear by people who will not bother to find out or even wonder about their true characters. Black youths are at the mercy of people with far more power and authority than they can muster and, as such, they are especially susceptible to punishment for their nonconformity. The proof of this disadvantage is cemented in statistics galore, from rates of arrest and incarceration, school suspensions, unemployment, and racial profiling.

The young folks have developed their own lingo and language codes, too, but this is hardly unusual for adolescents and teenagers, regardless of race. It got out of hand a few years ago in Oakland, California, where school officials gave serious consideration to incorporating something called "Ebonics" into the curriculum. The course would have put slang—a purposeful manip- ulation of the English language—on par with poor diction and bad grammar, which are accidents of miseducation. Fortunately, for the children of Oakland, widespread public objections reduced the plan to ashes.

Though undaunted by the mainstream's censure and disap- provals, black youths pay a dear price for this waltz with indepen- dence. It is hard on parents to let them take the chances and assert their individuality. Only on faith and trust do we let them go. Faith that their boldness will change the world. Trust in their right to try.

Another cause of black alienation is the outlandish theory that any disparities in our social and economic standing, compared to whites, are the result of moral torpor. If only we were more law- ful, more chaste, more prudent, and more industrious, goes this deception, then providence would smile on us. Anecdotal and sys- tematic racism are not factored into the equation.

Despite the iconoclasm of the youth culture, a hefty body of polls and studies conclude that black people are, by and large, staunch traditionalists. This is often mistaken for conservatism, but that is a mishap of the current political climate that insists on dividing everyone into conservative or liberal camps with little room for gradations or nuances. Even though black Americans hold varied opinions on political, fiscal, and social issues, the base- line values that inform those opinions are generally old-fashioned.

We believe in family, church, education, community, though not necessarily in that order. We believe in love and marriage, notwithstanding the fragile conditions of both these days. (In the 1930s, 94 percent of black women were married. Now, only 70 percent of the current crop of marriageable women are likely to wed. And the divorce rate, society-wide, is around 50 percent. Part of the reason may be that the availability of marriageable black men has been sharply reduced by imprisonment, disease, and premature death.)

Like other ethnic groups, we care deeply for children. Our commitment to the improvement of their lives is total. We agree that sound, supportive families, good health, safe neighborhoods and schools, caring teachers, well-rounded curricula, stimulating recreation, artistic expression, spiritual development, and civic involvement are essential to our children's well-being and how they see themselves and their possibilities.

But, in general, we part ways with many of the modern theories of child-rearing. In the main, we hold to our mothers' and fathers' models, demanding strict obedience from our children. Sociologists call this the "authoritarian" approach to parenting, and their studies show that it is commonly practiced in black households. In this arrangement, there is no counting to ten, no "time outs," no contracts between parent and child in order to secure compliance. We do not regard or treat them as peers and our homes are not democracies. We do not tolerate sassy mouths or defiant tones of voice. Inflicting corporal punishment—the subject of much consternation in these modern times—is considered a parental prerogative in most black families. Although it can certainly be overdone, our children seem to understand the difference between discipline and abuse. It is no trauma for us, not when the hand that swats is the same one that soothes. Tough love proved our parents cared enough to teach us about consequences and to arrest our bad behavior before those consequences worsened. It affirmed that they had inherited the sublime blend of tenderness and toughness that made their ancestors so wondrous. Besides, we understood that they were the most merciful judge and jury we were likely to face. The outside world would be much harsher in both the rules it imposed and the punishment it dispensed.

Many black households also hold to the tradition of male supremacy. But many black men are egalitarians and, generally, black women subscribe to feminist ideals, even if some are reluctant to enunciate them. It should be noted that the black feminist is often distinguishable from her white sisters by more than just ethnicity. There are characteristics that distinguish black feminists from our white counterparts. We recognize the black man as part of our struggle, so concern for our rights does not supercede concern for his. We are not offended by his cool, not afraid of his heat, not resentful of his swagger, not perturbed by his refusal to bow in the face of setbacks, not intimidated by his quest for power. He is not our oppressor, nor is he our competitor, but rather, he is our partner, a fellow soldier bombarded by stereotypes and suppositions, trying to maintain his balance and his hope under fire. Although the two are not mutually exclusive, the women's rights movement and the overarching black rights movement are thinly delineated, and it is a trick to walk that line without seeming to favor one side. As Duann Logwood, a young feminist, once stated, "I know that if I stood up in front of a black audience and declared myself a feminist, I would also have to explain that I was the type of feminist that fights for both civil rights and women's rights." At the same time, Duann adds, "There's a 'ghetto' of women like me whose issues are ignored and experiences marginalized by mainstream feminism. Much like people in the literal ghetto, we are a disunified mass lacking large support networks and a name that reflects our experience." So Logwood invented one: Ghetto Feminism. The feminist establishment has yet to recognize this branch of the movement. They only wonder why we are not more front and center.

It is a mistake to read this standoffishness as disinterest or ignorance about women's rights. Our history should be testament enough to our conviction that women are ready, willing, and able to lead and excel. But black rights are interwoven in that campaign—indeed, the American women's movement owes its existence to the abolitionist movement—and we know that the thread of women's rights cannot be plucked from the tapestry of civil rights without damaging the fabric. Barbara Smith, the noted black feminist author and activist, says black women do not have the organizational heft, the time, or the money to engage in "movement" activities. Whatever the reason for our underrepresentation on the front lines of feminism, our moral support is solid. We may not talk the talk, but we surely walk the walk.

As traditionalists, we are in for a tough fight. Modernity is a hard-nosed foe and it has claimed many victories over old-fangled ways. Like other subcultures, black America has surrendered a lot of the old tried and true to new standards that are counter to our customs and sensibilities. Despite accusations of tribalism and separatism, we have shelved many of the old ways and become disciples of the new. Like most Americans, we are ruled by pop culture. And like most, we are slowly losing our hold on heritage and the traditions that once distinguished us from the pack. Slowly but surely, our Americanism is burying our Africanism. There should be no penalty for trying to hold on to a piece of home.

Chapter 14

Census, Sense Us

Settling the race question once and for all may be even more difficult now that, for the first time in that nation's history, black Americans will not constitute the largest minority. The Latino population is swiftly taking over that position and the nation's institutions are making accommodations for this new "majority minority." What this bodes for the unfinished agenda of black America is worrisome. Without the weight of numbers behind us, white America—who will still hold most of the power—may take black American equality as a write-off.

We got a glimpse of this possibility on Election Day 2000, when Americans went to the polls to decide whether Texas governor George W. Bush, a Republican, or Vice President Albert Gore, a Democrat, should be the nation's forty-third president. The race was unusually close; every vote mattered. Indeed, it was so close that, as election night news coverage crossed into the wee hours of the next morning, the new presidency hung in the balance, hinging on Florida's decision.

But Florida had serious problems. Allegedly, some shady doings had taken place in the Sunshine State; "voting irregularities" is what election officials called them. Black Florida voters had a bushel basket of claims against the system. Having turned out in astonishing numbers—by some estimates, black voter turnout was 70 percent higher in 2000 than in 1996—some voters said they were harassed at the polling place, or refused voting privileges, or told they were listed as felons and were therefore ineligible to vote. To them, the "irregularities" must have been painfully familiar—a modern version of the poll tax, literacy test, and how-many-bubbles-in-a-bar-of-Ivory-soap devices.

Because of problems with some ballots that were cast and counted, thousands of Florida's votes were invalidated. Interestingly, 54 percent of the rejected ballots were cast by black voters, who accounted for only 11 percent of all Floridians who voted that day. Although the news media reported the claims, the allegations were generally dismissed as exaggerations, outright lies, or paranoia. The N.A.A.C.P. took them seriously, conducting hearings and gathering considerable credible evidence to prove something was rotten in Florida on November 7, 2000. Capitol Hill gave lip service to so-called election reform, but, with the exception of the Congressional Black Caucus and some Democrats, the issue failed to captivate the Congress. The White House, with George W. Bush installed in the Oval Office, wouldn't touch the issue, not when it was a foregone conclusion that all or nearly all of the discounted black votes would have gone to Gore—possibly enough to have elected him.

In June 2001, the U.S. Commission on Civil Rights concluded six months of investigation and issued a damning report. Florida's election conduct had been rife with "injustice, ineptitude and inefficiency" that had hit minority voters especially hard, the commission found. The report said black voters' ballots were rejected nearly ten times more often than white voters' ballots.

While the black vote is being written off by the Republican Party and taken for granted by the Democrats, both major political parties are breaking their necks to woo Latinos, the fastest growing ethnic group in the country. In terms of political payoffs, it makes sense to go after a population that is expanding and that tends to show up regularly at the polls. So, black Americans should hold no animosity toward Latinos, the beneficiaries of these courtships. But the political community may be in for a surprise if it thinks the black vote is passé. It is still large enough to swing many key elections and black Americans intend to use it to suit our needs and interests. Further, we have not forgotten that we were the ones who kicked the doors open for nonwhites in America, often at the cost of our lives and livelihoods. We are not about to be pushed to the back of the line now. After all, our progress has been considerable. No one needs numbers to prove that, it is obvious. But the numbers are certainly there—in the rise in black businesses and college graduates, the increase in black net worth and disposable income, the hike in black elected officials from three hundred in 1964 to more than nine thousand now. There is proof too in the popularity of black entertainment, art, scholarship, and literature, in the free-flowing commingling of races. The manifest progress is so conspicuous and considerable that it is incontestable, as impossible to deny as an elephant in the living room.

But when one considers where black people should have been in 1619 with the original landing at Jamestown, Virginia—which is to say, free and of equal standing—the country's self-congratulations and relief are premature. As has been said before, there is much left to be done and the work ahead of us will require elbow grease.

In order to make amends, the nation must first prove itself repentant. But, as we learned in 1997, that's easier said than done. It was then that a few white and black members of Congress proposed that the United States government apologize for slavery and the government's collusion in it. The proposal was roundly attacked by white Americans who disclaimed any responsibility for the long-gone institution or indebtedness of any sort to slaves' descendants. A war of words rolled across the country erupting in skirmishes at water coolers, country clubs, editorial boards, and the upper echelons of government and academe. Writing for the Ayn Rand Institute, Robert Tracinski issued a typical criticism.

> *An apology for slavery on behalf of the nation presumes that whites today, who predominantly oppose racism and never owned slaves, and who bear no personal responsibility for slavery, still bear a collective responsibility—a guilt they bear simply by belonging to the same race as the slave-holders of the Old South. Such an apology promotes the very idea at the root of slavery: racial collectivism.*

Apparently, it either did not occur or did not matter to opponents that the government is a continuum and that, when it speaks or acts, it does so in the name of all citizens, not just white ones. A ready apology would have spoken volumes about where the country's heart is. When it became clear—quickly—that no consensus would gather around the apology proposal, the idea withered on the vine. That was a telling act of omission. If white America was so preoccupied with the appearance of righteousness, so wrapped up in its own exoneration that it would sacrifice the goodwill and faith of thirty-five million of its people before it would utter the simple words, "I'm sorry," then how could anyone expect a commitment to the difficult and dirty work of real repair?

Even after that failure, some continue to promote the proposal that black Americans should be compensated for the wages and advantages lost to slavery and racism. Some plans call for cash payouts. More comprehensive measures would require appropriations of public funds and special programs designed to accelerate black progress until we stand where we would or should have, had discrimination never raised its hideous head. There are some reasonable, defensible, feasible plans out there, but I do not hold much hope for a systematic response to these demands for parity. The apology experiment was quite instructive as a predictor of how more dramatic remedies might fare.

A host of white folks seem to think our protestations are ridiculous and ungracious. In their judgment, slavery was, in the final analysis, a rescue effort, seminal to our improvement. "Now get down on your knees and thank God that your ancestors were slaves that were brought to this country and that you don't live in Africa!" reads a letter from one of my readers. "They really have problems there; yours are ridiculously minuscule by comparison. If you don't believe me, go there and stay." This is a popular twist on history, reiterated by angry newspaper readers, clergy, historians, and scholars. Usually, the argument is fastened to a deplorable aspect of African history that conveyors, like this reader from Knoxville,

Tennessee, are quick to recall. "Black people were selling black people into slavery in Africa long before Columbus discovered America," she wrote. "It was white Christian abolitionists in America and white Christian European males who invaded Africa and put a stop to the ancient practice of slavery and the genocide of one African tribe against another. Yet, one hundred years later, these same liberators were demonized as imperialists who were out to loot Africa's wealth and were forced to withdraw from the continent."

Close, but no cigar. "White Christian abolitionists in America" had little influence over the slave trade either of or by Africans. "The ancient practice of slavery" among African tribes did not usually involve lifelong involuntary servitude, but was an element of intertribal warfare and competition. "White Christian European males" did indeed invade and colonize Africa, but their role as arbitrators in intertribal slavery and certainly as destroyers of genocide was anecdotal, at best. The truth is that white European males, Christian or not, came most often to plunder Africa, not to save it.

Even some of the folks who wouldn't dream of defending the colonialists' and explorers' treatment of Africa and her peoples have nonetheless fallen into the bash-Africa trap, attacking the continent as a place to avoid. Once again, the gratitude theme hitches to this bandwagon, as seen in the following excerpt from *Politically Incorrect,* a popular late-night talk show hosted by comedian Bill Maher. The guests on the program that aired July 13, 2000, were Tavis Smiley, author and then-host of *BET Tonight* on Black Entertainment Television; Michael Graham, Republican political consultant and talk radio host from Charleston, South Carolina; comedian Cory Kahaney; and Cynthia Garrett, then host of NBC's

Later show. At the top of the show, Maher introduced the topic of reparations and an apology for slavery.

> *Smiley: Nobody complains about reparations or recompense or verdicts unless we're starting to talk about slavery. When everybody else gets paid—*
>
> *Graham: You have not been wronged by slavery. You've been treated well by slavery. You are fortunate today because three hundred years ago, your unfortunate ancestors went through a terrible, terrible, horrible experience. But it was a net win for you in your life because there are peoples whose ancestors weren't treated this terrible, terrible way and they're living in the poorest place in the world where the annual income is five bucks a year. I'm sorry.*
>
> *Maher: There's a book, I can't remember the guy's name. It's a black author, so don't look at me like that. He basically said the same thing, which is, in your heart of hearts, you're glad your ancestors made the trip because you do not want to live in Liberia.*
>
> *Graham: In 1860, people in the North, white people in the North, who had no issue in slavery at all went down and got killed and killed my relatives in the South—as they should have. It was a good thing for them to do to end slavery.*

Smiley later challenged Maher and the others when they lampooned Africa. Unlike Tavis, none of the others had visited the continent.

> *Smiley: It's not right for us to sit here and denigrate African countries. There are a lot of beautiful countries in Africa.*
>
> *Maher: No there are not.*

Smiley: No kidding. When was the last time you were in Africa?

Maher: I don't have to go to Africa. I have a thing called "CNN" in my house. It brings Africa right into my living room.

Still later in the show, Smiley and Maher had this exchange:

Smiley: We can't denigrate an entire continent. The reason why Bill Clinton went to Africa—

Maher: We're not denigrating, we're characterizing with reality. We're keeping it real on Africa.

Smiley: Keeping it real? My only point is, let's keep it real about Africa. Tell the good side and tell the bad side. America has the same problems, Bill.

Maher: It does not have the same problems. The electricity here does not go out at eight o'clock at night. There are not thugs running—

Smiley: Electricity doesn't go out in Beverly Hills, where you live.

It may have been inadvertent, but with his comments on that particular show, the proud iconoclast Bill Maher fell in league with a doctrinaire crowd—a crowd that includes M. Lester O'Shea, the previously discussed author of a book decrying government remedies for discrimination and economic disparity. O'Shea's take on African Americans' status? "It is true that they [are] in a more advanced condition than would have been the case had their ancestors not been taken from Africa and brought to America."

I can't imagine that O'Shea is Maher's kind of guy. But the Western and Eurocentric chauvinism they have both expressed makes them brothers, just as it binds millions of white Americans who might have little else in common ideologically.

Black people do not deny and offer no defense of the baleful practice of slavery. We find no relief in the fact that black human beings were the captors and traders of black human beings. But we are not swayed by the "gratitude" balderdash, being ever mindful of the laws of supply and demand as encapsulated in an eighteenth-century essay by Ottobah Cugoano, a freed slave. "To the shame of my own countrymen . . . I was first kidnapped and betrayed by my own complexion, who were the first cause of my exile and slavery," he wrote. "But if there were no buyers there would be no sellers." So much for the superiority of white morality and goodness. UCLA professor McLaren refers to revisionism about the origins and course of slavery as "social amnesia." It might work if everyone had it. But black Americans cannot forget how ours came to be the only ethnic group that did not come to America of its own free will. And we are not distracted from the real purpose behind our ancestors' forceful removal from the homeland. It was not done for our sakes, that's for damn sure.

For sport, let's extrapolate the "rescue" argument. If blacks should be thankful for having been snatched from home, then America should be appreciative toward black Americans because of our extensive contributions to the country's construction, defense, and prosperity. Not only did black men, women, and children tend the fields and waterways that fueled American commerce; not only did blacks build many of the mansions, the schools, the churches, and the monuments to government that America so proudly ex-tols—the U.S. Capitol and the White House among them—but these laborers allowed whites the luxury of busying themselves with other pursuits, like those that gave rise to the country's vaunted middle class in the early twentieth century. Until then, there was no middle class to speak of. Most white Americans scratched out a living either from the land or at a factory or foundry. A relatively and envied few lived like kings with hoarded wealth. Black and immigrant workers liberated the aspirations of working-class whites, allowing them to branch into other areas while someone else took care of their children and life's basic provisions. Thus, between 1900 and 1920, professionalism burgeoned. The number of people—white people—in advertising, civil engineering, secretarial and clerical fields, and other office-bound professions zoomed from 5.1 million to 10.5 million. Although most white wives and mothers did not have paid jobs then, 54 percent of urban black women worked, as domestics, seamstresses, or laundry women. That was in the city. Two-thirds of the country's black population remained in the rural South, usually dependent on sharecropping and tenant farming, a hand-to-mouth operation in which the entire family worked land, that typically belonged to whites, in exchange for food and housing. Others worked in tobacco and cotton plants for meager wages. Therefore, if America owes its reputation and security to robust and fruitful capitalism, then it owes a good part of that success to black enterprise and skill. So, let's not get into who did whom what favors.

In the absence of collective repentance, and in light of the shortcomings of public policy, the prospects for improved interracial relations rest with one-on-one mechanics. They may lack the power and speed of class action, but individual endeavor is at least movement and that is better than the steady state. Comes the question, then, what can one person do?

The first step is to take an inventory of one's own ideology. Think of yourself as having started out with a binder of blank pages. The pages begin filling in with instructions and pointers and observations. Mama writes upon the pages. Papa too. Aunts and neighbors and cousins and schoolmates provide passages. Teachers and ministers and store clerks have input. There are notes about things you heard or thought you heard and about what you saw or thought you saw. Whole lines are copied from books and songs and folklore. Guesswork and the imagination have had their say. After a while, your blueprint is a complete work. Now you have your how-to, what-to, why-to handbook of life.

We all play by the book to some degree. But the more reflective ones of us will occasionally pull the journal out, dust it off, and study the pages to see what revisions are in order. Maybe the memo from Grandma needs work. Perhaps we might change a word or two in the part we got from Miss What's-Her-Name in third grade. Could be that a whole section should be erased. Water under the bridge, common sense, vision, and honesty should cause us to challenge, change, or give up on the old rules from time to time. It is a pity and a shame, a stain on our intellect and decency, when we stick to the book without ever questioning it.

Says the scholar and writer Peter McLaren, in *White Reign*:

The logics of empire are still with us, bound to the fabric of our daily being-in-the-world; woven into our posture toward others, connected to the muscles of our eyes; dipped in the relations that excite and calm us; structured in the language of our perception. We cannot will our racist logics away. We need to struggle with a formidable resolve in order to overcome that which we are afraid

*to confirm exists let alone confront in the battleground of our
souls.*

Doug, a white man, is a dear friend from Belzoni, Mississippi.
He was a student at Ole Miss when James Meredith, a black student, arrived there in 1963 to register for classes—the first black
student to invade the cherished, magnolia-lined campus. When
riots and violence broke out among students and townspeople determined to keep the school lily-white, Doug was in the crowd,
throwing bottles, shouting epithets, and setting fires. It was his
programming, he once told me, to resist desegregation and de-
fend the doctrine of white supremacy and racial separatism. But,
as the school year progressed, with James Meredith in attendance
along with a swarm of federal marshals, Doug's new experiences
mocked his old fears and hatred. He began editing his handbook.
Over the years, Doug has thoroughly rewritten the original sec-
tions on race. He is open and friendly to good people from all
races, no longer hidebound and afraid and angry, and perfectly
willing to admit he had been wrong. The process, he says, has
made him a free man.

It is not easy. The temptation to fall back onto the warm cushions of familiarity and group think makes the editing all the more
difficult. Willpower is tough to maintain. The torrent of false or
misleading images is hard to resist. But stay the course and you will
see that the Creator did not err. While He gave human beings do-
minion over all other life, He did not set one mortal, willful life
above another. The human is a complex organism, but singular in
form regardless of ethnic origin. However we may dicker about
heritage and culture, anthropologists and biologists agree on this

blunt truth: The human species is simply not old enough to have developed any significant or fundamental differences among races. In other words, the differences in our behavior, attitudes, and customs are circumstantial. God did not make "thems"; that's our doing.

The emancipated will tell you that the grueling effort is worthwhile. With a new edition of the handbook, we will most certainly lose our fear of "others" because others will no longer exist. Which means we need not run or flinch or fume like we used to. We don't have to relocate because of our new neighbors; they no longer disturb us on sight. We don't have to drive our kids to private schools several miles away; the public school nearby will be just fine now that "others" don't scare us anymore and we've committed our spirits and resources to keeping the local school aloft. We no longer have to worry that we might miss the best friend, best partner, best coworker we could ever ask for, because now the pool of prospects is the whole world, not just the pen to which our options were once confined. Rewriting the book can be liberating indeed.

The "struggle" McLaren refers to would include respecting one another's subcultural traditions. We could expect even faster healing of our racial wounds if we joined, at least occasionally, in the practice or celebration of those traditions. We know how, as evidenced by the annual response to St. Patrick's Day. It is an Irish commemoration, but people of every ethnicity don green clothing and shamrock-shaped pins in tribute.

Black History Month is commemorated every February, which cynics like to point out is the calendar's shortest month. It is a petty point and a misguided grievance, considering the month was selected by Dr. Carter G. Woodson, a black educator and statesman, when he conceived Negro History Week in tribute to black contributions to the American story. Woodson chose February because it was the birth month of both Frederick Douglass, the redoubtable black abolitionist and orator, and President Abraham Lincoln whose less-than-enthusiastic championship of black emancipation was nonetheless inspired and effectual. In 1976, the commemoration was expanded and renamed Black History Month.

Every year, the occasion is greeted by a heap of special television programs, books, school projects, and symposia. It seems they have made a difference. More and more history and literature texts now include black accomplishments, developments, and works.

Ironically, some white Americans still believe slavery is the prime mover of black history and that Black History Month is, therefore, an excuse for dredging up past disgrace and residual anger. In my junior year of high school, black students staged an extravaganza for what was then still Negro History Week. The centerpiece of the all-school assembly marking the occasion was a play, written and choreographed by a black teacher, that embodied the timeline of black American life. The performance featured colorful African costumes, rich spirituals and instrumentation, and impressive, detailed scenery. It was a proud moment.

At the conclusion of the assembly, black students in the audience rose to their feet with wild applause. Many white students joined them. Others sat on their hands. We were disappointed but not totally surprised. We were not prepared, however, for the band of students who began singing "Dixie," eventually drowning out the ovation. That was in 1970.

Here is how ethnic celebrations were received at a racially mixed high school in tony Bethesda, Maryland, nearly three decades later. Consider the following excerpt from a letter to the school newspaper. It was signed by two white male students.

When the long awaited end comes to this month, the Caucasians have eight to rest until the guard goes back up when we're in October and it's Spanish Heritage Month. Our school went all out this year and brought in a Spanish comedian. This show greatly benefited no one. Or almost no one that is. His jokes were graciously in English but the actual punch lines were in Spanish. A whopping twelve percent of the population was having a great time, but unfortunately they were the only ones. Most everyone else sat politely in their chairs snoring in harmony. Though this month doesn't squeeze too much lemon juice in our healing paper cuts, they still have this one little complaint. "It's too much trouble to legally be a part of the United States." Hey get over it. This is our country that's yours. We don't keep you from coming in, as long as you do it legally. Finally, if it's socially acceptable for a black man to wear the "X" of Malcolm X, and if we are truly a society of fairness and equality, it should be just as socially acceptable to fly the Stars and Bars of the South and sing "Dixie" while watching her fly. All our lives everyone just wants to be treated equally. Do you really think giving a certain culture their own month is equal? If we're going to dedicate these months to minority groups, then let's call the other ten months White History Months.

The letter's authors are woefully misinformed. Among other errors, they wrote that "the black man has been no more oppressed than any other race who has migrated to this country"—a claim flawed in both its premise and its facts. We might blame lax instruction for the young writers' sorry command of history, but the bigotry underlying their argument was most likely learned as it was taught.

Toni Morrison, the Nobel Prize-winning author, says the transmission of racist passions is not only a disservice to youngsters, but a devastation. "Everybody remembers the first time they were taught that part of the human race was Other," Morrison once said in an interview with *Time* magazine. "That's a trauma. It's as though I told you that your left hand is not part of your body."

Certainly America can do a better job of honoring the assorted heritages it comprises. It can start by recognizing the purpose and benefits of such commemorations. They should not be used as appeasement. They should not be offered as pacifiers to quiet ethnological needs. A Spanish Heritage Month assembly featuring a Latino comedian is all right as part of the month's lineup, but if that was the sole event, it was cheap, gimmicky, and patronizing— a mockery of the occasion. Furthermore, it could not have edified non-Latinos who, believe me, beg enlightenment. The boys' letter underscores the point. "Most everyone else sat politely in their chairs snoring in harmony," it said. We want America's undivided attention, not her forbearance.

We must also be on the lookout for subtleties in legislation, policy, and covenants that encourage, install, or enforce discrimination. Closing off the passageways to the American Dream may not concern those already in the pipeline of power and privilege, but sooner or later, such cupidity will cost them. The nation's peace and prosperity require all hands on deck. Prolonged, widespread exclusion can only disable America. You would think morality alone could bring us around. If not that, then fidelity to the American creed should do it. But if nothing else moves us to do right, enlightened self-interest should suffice. Of course, it takes probity and reflection to reach enlightenment and, to the comfortable conservators of the status quo, that is nuisance work.

While much of the nation's attention to racism is focused on the shocking, the real threat to interracial harmony is the casual act of discrimination or insensitivity—that often unthinking, almost instinctive word or deed. A respected black newspaper columnist and commentator told me about one such experience.

One day, on an early morning cross-country flight, the attendant presented her pleasant face to the columnist and his seat mate. "For breakfast this morning, you have a choice of French toast or an omelet," she said. "Which would you like?"

Both men chose French toast. A few minutes later, the flight attendant returned with two covered dishes. The white passenger had French toast. The black columnist had an omelet.

"Excuse me," said the columnist. "But I ordered the French toast."

"I know," said the attendant. "But there was only one left."

The columnist will be the first to tell you that you don't go to war over French toast and omelets. But it is the underlying idea that crinkles good faith. It's the same idea that favors the white job candidate, the white college applicant, the white contractor, the white physician, and the white home-buyer over the nonwhite ones. It is not necessarily calculated or even cognitive. It probably has nothing to do with a plan, an intention, or a conspiracy. It is more like a reflex—like the bat of an eyelid reacting to some wee, silent order.

There is only one left. And of course, you won't mind that the white guy gets it.

Even the small bumps count. Add them up, keep them coming, and before you know it, a mountain is made.

Chapter 15

Reclamation

The force of Eurocentric standards has accomplished what even the monstrousness of slavery could not: it has ripped the hem of the black community, leaving it to unravel, strand by stand. Even in slavery, we did not kill one another, did not abandon our children, did not abide idleness, did not squander education, did not leave the church, did not look the other way when our neighbors were in want. Even during the lynch-happy years, the age of the night riders and the era of Jim Crow, we did not forsake our duty to ourselves and to one another. Ironically, the demise of the black community as we knew it can be traced to the advent of desegregation. I would never suggest that segregation was better, but the increase in income and other standards of "success" that came with its undoing are not enough to compensate for the loss of our integrity and the wreckage that has occurred.

It is not a lost cause, however. We can recover. We can rebuild and we must. But reconstruction will be long and hard. The clock is ticking. It is time to regroup.

My proposal is bound to throw some Americans into a conniption, but I hope most will consider it before tossing it aside as separatist claptrap. I do not offer these recommendations to repudiate white America, but with an eye on the dire and urgent needs of black Americans whose salvation is overdue.

Where desegregation has succeeded, integration has not materialized and assimilation is a failed proposition in that it requires subjugation, or denial, of heritage's dictates. The American Way may be singular in theory, but in practice it must be multifaceted. Efforts to equalize those variances have been stymied by white domination, creating tragedies and festering ill will among those who have not, can not, and should not be required to wholly conform.

Restoring the black community to its original state may not be feasible given the mobility and sprawl of modern society. The Ninth Streets of America may be gone for good. But we can all move to the same neighborhood spiritually and, from that place, we can erect monuments to our heritage.

The steps to rebuilding include:

- Patronage of historically black colleges and universities, where our children can get the education they need while taking a vacation from racism. The benefits of such relaxation are long-ranged. Without having to contend with racial prejudices day in and day out for a few years, young minds tend to stretch and grow, self-confidence blossoms and a sense of fraternity, of belonging, flourishes. When they return to the outer world, they are intellectually and emotionally stronger, undaunted by the competition and, usually, raring to test their mettle.

- Creation of co-ops, coalitions, and networks whereby black money, energy, talent, and other resources are pooled. Consolidation and synergy can make a difference in black holdings, from farms to banks to schools. It can also increase political clout, which will be in great demand as the nation's demographics change in the wake of immigration and fluctuating birth rates.

  For this, we could take a lesson from Mrs. Leonard Thomas of Washington, D.C., who, one day, got fed up with the run-down apartment complex she was living in. She and her neighbors petitioned their landlord to repair the place, but he ignored them. Mrs. Thomas and her fellow tenants dug up a city ordinance that allowed them to buy the building and convert it into a cooperative. The Lightview Cooperative is now ten years old. The people who live there are no longer renters, but home-owners. Together, the units are worth more than $700,000, twice what it cost to buy them. That's the kind of teamwork that can put black Americans on the road to financial security and all its perks.

- Gathering and guarding the children. The village model, in which every adult is vested with authority to chastise and correct all children and the responsibility to protect and nourish them, carries a certain risk nowadays that was rarely seen in old times. Parents have been known to react angrily, even violently, to outside interventions. Thus, many people have washed their hands of the duty out of fear or disgust.

The children have been emboldened by the limits this puts on their accountability. As a result, more children take license to impudence and fewer people constrain it. The new community must let go of grudges and dread. It has to put its arms back around the children, both to embrace them and to give them the boundaries they need to feel, and be, secure.

- Reconnection with God. One of secular society's greatest deceits is its growing cynicism about divine authority. The more science and philosophy are able to explain worldly phenomena and human events, the livelier the doubt about the existence and power of God. Whatever our religion, black Americans are steeped in spirituality. But the faithfulness of the ancestors does not assure us a seat in heaven. There is no affirmative action program there. Each of us must make our own connection, seek our own mercy, obtain our own grace. The recognition of and service to a higher power must undergird the new black community if it is to stand.
- Perseverance. In the continuing civil rights debate, social conservatives frequently decry "the culture of victimization"—their term for grievances about the legacy of slavery and the durability of racism. Protest all they want, but the relationship between our history and our present conditions is manifest. It is inarguable that we have been, and continue to be, victims of assorted wrongdoing. We must track down and subdue the villain, bend him to justice and prevent him from doing further harm. But we cannot stop there. At some point, we have to pour our energies into moving on.

A lumberjack was working in the woods one day when a tree fell on him. Someone else had made a bad cut in the tree, causing it to topple in the wrong direction. For hours, the trapped man tried to free himself, but one leg was hopelessly stuck. As time passed, the man felt his life slipping away, so traumatic were his injuries. After it became clear that no help was coming, he pulled a knife from his pocket and did what he had to do. He amputated the trapped leg. It was a horrible choice, but it saved his life.

The man could have stayed under the tree, cursing his fate, cursing whoever it was that made the bad cut in the trunk, cursing the fact that no one seemed to care enough about his whereabouts to come looking for him. All of that would have been justifiable, understandable. It was not fair. It was someone else's fault. Someone should have come to his aid. But, had he concentrated only on blaming his circumstances, he would have surely died. Be a victim, but be a live one. Save what you can.

- Civic and political activism. Black people tend to flock to one major party or the other en masse. It has been our history to follow the party that speaks to our common concerns and interests. But, it is time for a new paradigm—actually, a not so new one: divide and conquer.

In order to leverage our weight as a power group, we need participants on all fronts. However, it is important that they be activists, not merely members. The political parties need some serious shaking up, not just another new face toeing the line. Some black Republicans are giving the old leadership the blues. That's good; agitation keeps the dust from settling. Every established political group needs to be knocked off their cushions. Black votes should be earned by the sweat of the brow. It's our job to turn up the heat.

- Devaluing things, revaluing people. In a 1996 article in the *Journal of Adolescence,* Robert J. Jagers reported the results of his study of low-income fifth- and sixth-graders and the incidence of delinquency. He found a correlation between the children's aggressive behavior and the pressure to attain material prosperity and to compete with one another. These Anglo-American precepts are fundamental to capitalism, which butters the bread. But when they become too important to us, they collide with our cultural directives to put spirituality, character, cooperation, and neighborliness first. I am not suggesting that we forsake materialism, only that we not participate in the American habit of hyperconsumerism, which borders on gluttony and corrupts our traditions. We should appreciate personal quality over personal possession.

The manifesto for the restored black community is, in effect, an enlargement of Kwanzaa, the annual December celebration of traditional African doctrines. Kwanzaa was established in 1966 by Dr. Maulana Karenga, a professor at California State University in Long Beach. Even among black Americans, Kwanzaa is often mistaken as a substitute for Christmas. It is not. Karenga wisely created it to coincide with Christmas in order to take advantage of its family-oriented, gift-giving, and reflective spirit. Kwanzaa promotes seven principles: unity, self-determination, collective work and responsibility, cooperative economics, purpose, creativity, and faith—worthy endeavors, year-round, twenty-four/seven.

The yield from such an effort will be magnificent. Within the context of the seven principles, we can complete the unfinished business of freedom by making a place to stretch our legs, to exercise, test and increase our skills and talents, to revel in and reward our accomplishments, to pass something on to our children.

Let us raise our sights, raise awareness, raise Cain occasionally. But most of all, let us raise the village. Then, the United States will be, at last, a place that feels like home.

References

Aizenman, Nurith C., "In Bowie, Race is on the Agenda," *Washington Post*, B1, April 9, 2001.

"Armed Forces Equal Opportunity Survey," U.S. Department of Defense, November 1997.

Bacon, John, "Ex-paratrooper Gets Life in Killing of Black People," *USA Today*, 3A, May 7, 1997.

Benda, Julien, *La Traison des clercs*, New York: William Morrow & Co., 1928.

Berliner, Michael S., and Gary Hull, "Diversity and Multiculturalism: The New Racism," Ayn Rand Institute, www.aynrandinstitute/medialink/diversity.html.

"The Black Population in the United States, March 1999," U.S. Bureau of Census, November 2000.

Blakemore, Edward, "The Effect of Mandatory Minimum Sentencing on Black Males and the Black Community," University of Dayton School of Law, 1999.

Boston, Thomas D., *Affirmative Action and Black Entrepreneurship*, London and New York: The Century Foundation, 1999.

Bowen, William G., and Derek Bok, *The Shape of the River: Long*

Term Consequences of Considering Race in College and University Admission, Princeton, NH: Princeton University Press, 1998

Bundy, McGeorge, "The Issue Before the Court: Who Gets Ahead in America?," *Atlantic Monthly*, November 1977.

Campbell, Douglas A., Tom Avril, and Amy Worden, "New Jersey to Pay Four Men Shot at by Troopers," *Philadelphia Inquirer*, A1, February 3, 2001.

Claiborne, William, "Supremacist Group Grows Nationwide: Hate Crime Monitors Horrified by Spread of Organization Linked to 1999 Rampage," *Washington Post*, A3, June 29, 2000.

Cole, David, and John Lamberth, "The Fallacy of Racial Profiling," *New York Times*, Section 4, page 13, May 13, 2001.

Dedman, Bill, "Blacks turned down for home loans from S&Ls twice as often as whites," *Atlanta Journal-Constitution*, A1, January 22, 1989.

D'Souza Dinesh, *The End of Racism: Principles for a Multiracial Society*, New York: Simon and Shuster, 1996.

Entman, Robert M., and Andrew Rojecki, *The Black Image in the White Mind: Media and Race in America*, University of Chicago Press, 2000.

"Facing the Consequences: An Examination of Racial Discrimination in U.S. Public Schools," Applied Research Center, Oakland, CA, March 1, 2000.

"Family Sues Cincinnati," *Newsday*, A30, May 11, 2001.

Fletcher, Michael A., "Black Farmers May Get $1 Billion; Thousands to Share Settlement in Bias Suit," *Cleveland Plain Dealer*, 1C, June 23, 2000.

Gaston, Paul M., "Honor to the Class of '69: Reflections on Affirmative Action," University of Virginia, June 1999.

Gonzalez, David, "Counting the Vote: The Race Factor; Blacks Citing Flaws, Seek Inquiry into Florida Vote," *New York Times*, A13, November 11, 2000.

Grant, Donald, *The Way It Was in the South: Black Enterprise in Georgia*, New York: Birch Lane, 1993.

Grier, Peter, and James Skip Thurman, "Ruling May Clarify Affirmative Action," *Christian Science Monitor*, p. 3, March 10, 1998.

"Group Differences in Standardized Testing and Social Stratification Advancing Minority Achievement," The College Board, December 1999.

Hacker, Andrew, "Race: America's Rawest Nerve," Media Studies Journal, The Freedom Forum, 1994.

Hanley, Robert, "Whitman Said She Did Not Have Facts on Racial Profiling until '99," *New York Times*, B4, October 13, 2000.

Holzer, Harry J., "Career Advancement Prospects and Strategies for Low-Wage Minority Workers," The Urban Institute, March 2000.

"Innocence Protection Act of 2001 Section-By-Section Summary," News Release, National Association of Criminal Defense Lawyers, March 7, 2001.

Jagers, Robert J., "Culture and Problem Behaviors Among Inner City African American Youth: Further Explanation," *Journal of Adolescence*, 1996.

Jefferson, Thomas, "Notes on the State of Virginia," 1781–82.

Jerome, Morris E., "What Is the Future of Predominantly Black Urban Schools?: The Politics of Race in Urban Education Policy," *Phi Delta Kappan*, Vol. 81, No. 4, p. 316, December 1, 1999.

Joyner, Tammy, "Black Wealth: Inherent Disadvantage," *Atlanta Journal-Constitution*, October 30, 1995.

"Justice on Trial: Racial Disparities in the American Criminal Justice System," Leadership Conference on Civil Rights and Leadership Conference Education Fund, May 2000.

Katzenback, Nicholas, and Burke Marshall, "Not Color Blind: Just Blind," *New York Times*, Section 6, p. 42, February 22, 1998.

Kelley, Tina, "In Images of Jesus, Artists Transcend Crucifix," *New York Times*, April 30, 2000.

"Key Points: The Rally for Black Farmers and Small Family Farmers," News Release, Food First Institute for Food and Development Policy, May 8, 2000.

"Landmark Lawsuit on Behalf of Public School Students Demands Basic Education Rights Provided in State Constitution," American Civil Liberties Union News Release, May 17, 2000.

Larrubia, Evelyn, "Second Racist Gets Life for Murder; Courts: Skinhead Shouts Obscenities at Prosecutor, Investigator as Judge Sentences Him for Killing Homeless Man Because He Was Black," *Los Angeles Times*, B1, November 24, 1999.

Letter to President George W. Bush from Gary R. Grant, President, Black Farmers and Agriculturalists Association, March 29, 2001.

Lichtblau, Eric, "A Surprising Civil Rights About-Face for Ashcroft," *Los Angeles Times*, A1, May 13, 2001.

Lindsay, Sue, "Barnum Convicted of Racist Killing; Jurors Reject Argument that Former Skinhead Simply Watched His Pal Gun Down African Man," *Rocky Mountain News*, March 16, 1999.

Locke, Alaine, "Enter the New Negro," *The Survey Graphic*, Vol. VI, No. 6, March 1925.

Loury, Glenn C., "The Conservative Line on Race," *Atlantic Monthly*, 144–154, November 1997.

Mauer, Marc, "Lock 'Em Up and Throw Away the Key: African American Males and the Criminal Justice System," The Sentencing Project, 1999.

McAlpin, John P., "New Jersey Says Cops Still Look at Race," Associated Press, April 3, 2001.

McLaren, Peter, "Whiteness is . . . The Struggle for Postcolonial Hybridity," *White Reign: Deploying Whiteness in America*, New York: St. Martin's Press, 1998.

McMurray, Jefferey, "California Businessman Eyes Florida Affirmative Action Laws," *Naples Daily News*, January 22, 1999.

Montgomery, Lori, "Racial Profiling in Maryland Defies Definition—or Solution," *Washington Post*, A1, May 16, 2001.

Moynihan, Daniel Patrick, "The New Racialism," *Atlantic Monthly*, August 1968.

Myrdal, Gunnar, *An American Dilemma: The Negro Problem and Modern Democracy*, New York: Harper Brothers, 1944.

"The National Report Card on Discrimination," The Urban Institute, 1999.

Neal, Terry M., and David S. Broder, "Affirmative Action Tears at Florida GOP," *Washington Post*, A1, May 15, 1999.

Newkirk, Pamela T., "A Look at Black Journalists, White Media," *Washington Post*, September 24, 2000.

Newman, Maria, "Four Hundred Protest Racial Profiling, But Few Top Officials Hear," *New York Times*, B5, May 17, 2001.

Newport, Frank, "Whites Oppose Formal Apology for Slavery; Blacks Heavily in Favor," Gallup News Service, July 25, 1997.

O'Shea, M. Lester, *A Cure Worse Than the Disease: Fighting Dis-*

crimination Through Government Control, Tampa, FL: Hallberg Publishing, 1999.

Oliver, Melvin and Thomas Shapiro, *Black Wealth/White Wealth*, New York: Routledge Press, 1995.

Orfield, Gary, and John T. Yun, "Resegregation in American Schools," Civil Rights Project, Harvard University, June 1999.

Parker, Suzi, "The Vanishing Black Farmer," *Christian Science Monitor*, 1, July 13, 2000.

Peterson, Iver, "Panel Seeks Impeachment Proceedings Against Verniero," *New York Times*, April 12, 2001.

————, "Whitman Says Troopers Used Racial Profiling," *New York Times*, A1, April 21, 1999.

————, "Justice Dept. Switches Sides in Racial Case," *New York Times*, Section 1, p. 37, August 14, 1994

Poe-Yamagata, Eileen, and Michael A. Jones, "And Justice for Some," Youth Law Center, April 25, 2000.

Polednak, Anthony P., *Segregation, Poverty and Mortality in Urban African Americans*, New York: Oxford University Press, 1997.

"Prosecutor drops charges against man who spent 19 years in prison. DNA test results produce new suspect," Associated Press, May 3, 2001.

Racism in Medicine: The Legacy of Racial Bias and the Impact on African American Health," National Medical Association, March 1999.

"Reporter Frisked on Passer-By Error," Associated Press, May 23, 2000.

Ross, Sonya, "Clinton Orders Data on Racial Profiling," Associated Press, *Boston Globe*, A1, June 10, 1999.

Shapiro, Joseph P., "Heroes: Jim McCloskey; He has brought freedom to 25 innocent prisoners," *U.S. News and World Report*, 45–46, August 20/August 27, 2001.

"Soldier Gets Life in Racial Killings," *Pittsburgh Post-Gazette*, A5, May 13, 1997.

Southern Poverty Law Center, "The Year in Hate," www.splcenter.org, 1999.

"The State of Black America 1999," National Urban League, June 1999.

"The State of Black America 2000," National Urban League, June 2000.

"States required to provide adequate capital counsel, DNA testing; Innocence Protection Act addresses root of wrongful convictions," News Release, National Association of Criminal Defense Lawyers, March 7, 2001.

Steele, Claude M., "Race and the Schooling of Black Americans," *Atlantic Monthly*, April 1992.

Stout, David, "White House to Say School Was Wrong on Racial Issue," *New York Times*, B5, August 22, 1997.

Taylor, Quintard, *In Search of the Racial Frontier: African Americans in the American West, 1528–1990*, New York: W.W. Norton, 1998.

Thernstrom, Stephan and Abigail, *America in Black and White: One Nation, Indivisible*, New York: Simon and Shuster, 1997.

Tonry, Michael, *Malign Neglect*, New York: Oxford University Press, 1995.

Tracinski, Robert, "Apology for Slavery Will Perpetuate Racism," Ayn Rand Institute, www.aynrandinstitute/medialink/apology.html.

Transcript, Charlton Heston's Keynote Address to the Free Congress Foundation 20th Anniversary Gala, Washington, D.C., December 20, 1997.

Transcript, Interview with Ward Connerly, *Interracial Voice*, April 24, 1999.

Transcript, *Politically Incorrect*, ABC Television, July 13, 2000.

Transcript, "Bitter Harvest: Discrimination on the Farm," *News-Hour with Jim Lehrer*, PBS, 1998.

Transcript, Trial, *State of California Versus Orenthal James Simpson*, August 28, 1995.

"United Methodists Back African American Farmers," News Release, United Methodist General Conference, May 11, 2000.

U.S. Department of Health and Human Services, www.raceand-health.omhrc.gov.

West, Cornell, *Race Matters*, Boston: Beacon Press, 1993.

Wilson, William Julius, *When Work Disappears: The World of the New Urban Poor*, New York: Knopf, 1996.

Wise, Tim, "Color-Conscious, White-Blind: Race, Crime and Pathology in America," *LiP*, September/October 1998.

Zelnick, Bob, *Backfire: A Reporter's Look at Affirmative Action*, Washington, D.C.: Regnery Publishing, 1996.

Zinn, Howard, *A People's History of the United States, 1492–Present*, New York: HarperCollins, 1999.

Index

Index

Houston, Tex.:
  environmental racism and, 173
  history of black enterprise in, 164
Howard University, 182

Illinois, capital punishment in, 141
Imitation of Life, 192
infant mortality rates, 171
inheritances, 158, 162–62, 166
Initiative 200, 94
In Search of the Racial Frontier (Taylor), 163–64
integration, *see* desegregation
intelligence, academic racism and, 175–78, 181–82, 205
interracial harmony, 6, 8, 36, 217
  academic racism and, 175
  desegregation and, 53–55
  one-on-one mechanics of, 224–27, 230–31
  self-deception about, 21
Iverson, Allen, 198

Jagers, Robert J., 238
Jefferson, Thomas, 9–10, 170
Johnson, Andrew, 161
Johnson, Jim, 6–7
Johnson, Lyndon, 52, 166
Joint Center for Political and Economic Studies, 67
journalists, racial profiling and, 119
justice, justice system, 145–50
  affirmative action and, 99–101, 105, 108
  black defendants at disadvantage in, 146–50, 153–54
  desegregation and, 57
  drugs and, 145
  education and, 61–62, 70–71, 79–80
  juvenile crime and, 139–40
  King case and, 22–25, 27, 32, 35–36, 129
  racial profiling in, 114–16, 120, 129
  reclaiming community and, 236
  Simpson case and, 28–36, 147
Justice Policy Institute, 137
juvenile crime, 41, 133–40, 149

drug abuse and, 135, 145
statistics on, 137

Kahaney, Cory, 220
Karenga, Maulana, 238
"Keep Your Head Up," 207
Kemp, Jack, 95–96
Kennedy, John F., 100
Kennedy High School, 70
King, Martin Luther, Jr., 8, 201
King, Rodney, beating of, 22–25, 27, 32, 35–36, 129
Klebold, Dylan, 133–34, 136–38
Koon, Stacey, 22, 129
Korean War, 92
Ku Klux Klan, 106, 160–61
Kwanzaa, 238

Latinos, 185, 191, 215
  affirmative action and, 86, 93, 98, 104–6
  capital punishment and, 141
  celebrating history of, 229–30
  education and, 63, 65, 67–68, 71, 76, 93
  environmental racism and, 174
  juvenile crime and, 138–40
  prisons and, 152
  racial profiling and, 112, 114, 117, 130
  voting of, 217
Lee, Henry, 31
Lester, Peter, 164
Lincoln, Abraham, 7, 228
Little Rock, Ark., 53–60
  black community of, 38–49
  desegregation and, 39, 53–58, 60
  gangs in, 48–49
  juvenile crime in, 136
  public education in, 75, 83–85
Little Rock Central High, 39, 60
Locke, Alain, 3, 10
Locke, Edwin A., 179–82
Logwood, Duann, 211–12
Look, the, 15–19, 121
Los Angeles, Calif., 5, 21–28
  juvenile crime in, 136
  King beating and, 22–25

254